The Road Home

Sister Stan

TRANSWORLD IRELAND

TRANSWORLD IRELAND
An imprint of The Random House Group Limited
20 Vauxhall Bridge Road, London SW1V 2SA
www.transworldbooks.co.uk

THE ROAD HOME
A TRANSWORLD IRELAND BOOK: 9781848270602

First published in 2011 by Transworld Ireland
a division of Transworld Publishers
Transworld Ireland paperback edition published 2012

Addresses for Random House Group Ltd companies outside the UK
can be found at: www.randomhouse.co.uk
The Random House Group Ltd Reg. No. 954009

The Random House Group Limited supports The Forest Stewardship Council
(FSC®), the leading international forest-certification organisation. Our books carrying
the FSC label are printed on FSC®-certified paper. FSC is the only forest-certification
scheme endorsed by the leading environmental organisations, including Greenpeace.
Our paper-procurement policy can be found at www.randomhouse.co.uk/environment

Typeset in Granjon by Falcon Oast Graphic Art Ltd.
Printed and bound by CPI Group (UK) Ltd, Croydon, CR0 4YY.

2 4 6 8 10 9 7 5 3 1

MIX
Paper from
responsible sources
FSC® C016897

To be human
is to become visible
while carrying
what is hidden
as a gift to others.

David Whyte (from the poem *What to Remember When Waking*)

Acknowledgements

These thoughts were written not so much to find myself in a book, as simply to find myself. As I wrote I found myself drawn more and more into my inner journey and more attentive to my outward journey with many people and many places.

I hope it will bring hope and solace to those who need it on their own journey.

I would like to thank Treasa Coady and Siobhan Parkinson, who encouraged me to write this book in the first place, with very special thanks to Siobhan who gave me invaluable help with the text at the early stages. To Brenda Kimber, my editor, and Eoin McHugh at Transworld Ireland, for their careful and thorough work, and for their great respect for the book.

To Kathleen Clarke who typed various drafts of the book.

Finally I want to thank all those who have been a source of inspiration in my life, and who are all in this book – in one way or another, named and unnamed.

Contents

Foreword

by Mary McAleese, President of Ireland

The words of T.S. Eliot, 'Do not follow where the path may lead. Go instead where there is no path and leave a trail,' beautifully sum up the life journey of Sr Stanislaus Kennedy, whose wonderful work I have been privileged to witness on many occasions during my years as President of Ireland and indeed to share in long before I became President.

Sr Stanislaus – or Sr Stan as she has become affectionately known – is one of those rare people who knows that, in order to make life better for others, it is often necessary to choose the paths in life that are unfamiliar, difficult to navigate, and strewn with obstacles. Sr Stanislaus has never been afraid to set out down those demanding paths, to break new ground and to bring others with her. It is humbling to realize how, on many occasions, the only signposts she had to guide her came from her faith and from her heart and they told her to follow the voice of 'compassion', 'care', 'concern', 'empathy', 'kindness' and, of course, 'courage'. No matter where they led, she followed.

Sr Stan's determination to give her life to help the poor and the marginalized was awoken in a bleak, post-World-War, impoverished Ireland still coming to grips with a hard-fought-for independence. It was an Ireland navigating in uncharted waters as it moved from being a small, inward-looking country to a key player on the European stage, from being a land torn apart by conflict and violence to an island at peace, from being a mono-cultural country to one that people of all nationalities have chosen to call home. With each transformative phase the quality of life for many improved, but there has always been work to do for the poor and marginalized.

As the landscape changed, so too did the needs of our most vulnerable people and Sr Stanislaus kept pace with changing needs, outreaching to the homeless and to Ireland's new citizens from other parts of the world and encouraging the early development of a sense of social responsibility in our young people through her very successful Young Social Innovators initiative.

It would be impossible to measure fully the good that Sr Stan has done, the lives she has touched so graciously and caringly, the light of hope she has switched on for men, women and children who lived in the darkness of exclusion. 'Two shortens the road,' says the old Irish proverb, and that is what Sr Stan has done for a lot of people. She has walked with them, talked with them, listened to them and brought them to a better and a safer destination than might have seemed possible at the start.

It is hard to imagine Ireland without Sr Stanislaus's special charisma of care and her utter fidelity to the great commandment to love one another, which infuses all she does. I am proud to know her, proud to have worked with her and grateful to have such an inspirational champion of charity helping our country to fulfil its destiny as a republic that 'cherishes all the children of the nation equally'.

I wish her continued success as she navigates us closer to that destiny.

Mary McAleese
President of Ireland

1

Deora Dé

I was born Treasa Kennedy near Lispole on the Dingle peninsula in County Kerry in the south-west of Ireland, between Conor Hill and the Atlantic Ocean, during World War II – 1939 to be exact. That part of Kerry was partly Irish-speaking at the time. People are very proud to speak good Irish today, but in those days it was considered the language of poverty, and people tended to favour English. But I grew up in a household where Irish was spoken alongside English.

My family, like many local families, had its roots in Kerry for many generations. The Kennedys came to the Dingle peninsula from Tipperary in the middle of the eighteenth century. My father was Tadgh Mhuillean (Tadgh of the Mill), and was called that because his family owned a mill on the river in the nineteenth century. To this day where we live is called Mhuillean, even though its correct title is Rinn Bhui, the Yellow Hill, because of the abundance of montbretia that grows there. I was known as Treasa, one of Tadgh A. Mhuillean's daughters. Being able to identify a

1

place as somewhere you belong is something I took for granted as a child, but now it is very important to me, and the area I grew up in has left an indelible mark on my life. I love everything about the area: the community spirit, the football, the storytelling, the mountains and rivers and seas, the lakes and the valleys. It has an energy – a physical energy – which is the source of its language and its stories, its plays and poetry; it has a special accent and a certain toughness. Much of it is shaped by the landscape, and the landscape has a profound effect on its people.

I have a crystal-clear memory of how both the rising and the setting sun cast dancing lights on the hills; even after a shower of rain, everything seemed clearer – cleansed, in a way. Going back home now, and as I walk on Inch or Ventry Strand, I feel my childhood being reawakened through the sand, the sound of the waves, the smell of the sea and the wind and rain on my face; the beautiful shades of blues and greens, greys, yellows, purples. Now I can walk these strands with ease, and in all seasons, for every day different hues of nature appear to me.

I was one of six children (though my youngest brother died at birth) and I grew up among fishermen and farmers, the caretakers of a peasant tradition. I was very aware of the emigration and unemployment which did not allow many young people to live and work in the country, and I knew that most young people who didn't get into secondary school left Ireland in search of a better future.

My mother had emigrated to America as a young woman, but unusually she returned home. She enjoyed her time in America, but she knew that the immigrant life there was not what she wanted for her children, and she was absolutely determined that we would all be educated so that we could find work at home in Ireland.

In my early childhood, most of my entertainment came from simple games played in fields and roads; we would go to swim or paddle in the 'short strand' or climb the side of Conor Hill or the *strickeen*, which was at the back of our house, and though it was only a thousand feet, it felt as if it was several thousands. At night people gathered in the kitchen and the children of the house, who were supposed to be in bed, would sit on the stairs listening to the conversations going on below. At that time no one travelled too far out of the locality, unless it was to attend a hospital appointment or go to work in Dublin – or, of course, to emigrate.

And so the conversations tended to focus on local people and local events.

There was also storytelling and card-playing to be enjoyed in place of cinema, television or radio. It was a life of mystery, beauty and simplicity. The pattern of day and night, the rhythm of the seasons, of life and death – all this was lived unselfconsciously in the presence of God. The life of the people was deeply incarnational, as they saved the hay, cut and footed the turf (peat), brought tea to the fields or the bog, caught trout and salmon, told the time from the sun and the tide.

My first school was Lispole National School, which was a two-mile walk away, and when I left this school it was a very lonely time for me. I had made many, many friends and there was nobody from my class going to secondary school with me. At the same time, my three older sisters had left home and were training

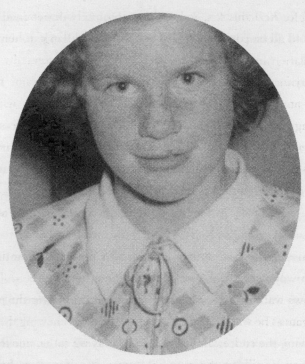

Me as a child, aged around eight or nine.

to be teachers or nurses. I was on my own at home, with my brother, who was two years younger than me. To me, he was just a very young child and I didn't want much to do with him. In fact, we seemed to spend most of our time squabbling! It was only when my sisters came home on holidays that things changed. They obviously regarded themselves as a bit more sophisticated than us because they were out in the world and we were still at school, so my brother and I became closer, and that was how it remained.

Going to secondary school meant riding three miles into town, in Dingle. And this I had to do on my own, without family or friends to accompany me. It was certainly a challenge to develop new relationships and find my feet in what was, essentially, foreign territory. But somehow I managed.

Life at home had a gentleness to it. I remember my mother bringing the eggs from the henhouse in her turned up, crossover apron, and how she would mindfully, gently, place them in a bowl in the kitchen. I remember, too, watching her kneading bread or carefully rolling out the pastry for the delicious apple tarts she baked. Nothing was rushed, or forced, just mindful, focused work that she seemed happy to do.

I can see now my father coming down the road, walking meditatively behind the cows as they came home to be milked. The cows walking so, so slowly. I see him leaning over the pillar of the gate as he watched and listened to the cows chewing the hay or chewing the cud; I can feel the stillness as we sat on our three-legged stools milking the cows. There was a calmness, a rhythm and a beauty to these simple tasks.

As a young child growing up on a farm, I watched my father work the land and spent a lot of time out of doors. This closeness to the land came from walking it and working it and, in a sense, I recognized early that satisfaction is easily achieved in farm life. There was satisfaction when the hay is saved, the corn is reaped and thrashed, the turf is cut, when the potatoes are set and picked, when the cow calves and the milk tanks are full. All of this comes, of course, from hard work, but it was a rich life, simplicity at its best, surrounded by nature and animals. One of the best aspects of my childhood was that we always had animals around us – calves,

My parents on the farm, taken around 1946.

horses, ponies, donkeys, sheep, goats – and all so much a part of our daily, hectic life. It was fun, and there was never a dull moment, but we knew too that living on a farm entailed certain responsibilities.

As children, we had to help with duties around the farm: saving the hay and the corn, footing the turf (a way of drying out the turf after it was cut), setting, weeding and picking the potatoes and other vegetables we grew. It was hard, tiring work, but we were shown how to do things properly and never deviated from that. For example, when we were setting the potatoes, after the sod was turned over we all had our own place beside the ridge and were taught how to place the seed potatoes in a certain way, with the eye facing up and at a certain distance from each other along the ridge. Saving the hay was a great event we all helped with. But the weather had to be fine. I remember when the weather was bad, the priest gave permission from the altar allowing farmers to work on Sunday.

There was much excitement about the place when the neighbours gathered to help each other bring home the turf or stack the hay. The hay was brought in from the fields at the end of the summer on carts drawn by horses, and stacked in one big stack in the yard. We had so much fun going back and forth on the cart!

Another enjoyable occasion was the American Wakes. The American Wake was a carry over from a long tradition of emigration in the area. It dates back to the earlier part of the twentieth century, a time of high emigration to America. At that time, few emigrants to America were expected to return, so a big party was held in the area before they left, to Wake them, as it were, and send them on their journey. This was a big occasion for food, drink and music, singing and dancing. There was also lovely food and drinks for the children. During my childhood the American Wakes were generally held when Americans were returning to the States after their holiday in Ireland.

Like all youngsters I lived for the moment, the fun, the games, the visiting of neighbours and cousins, and other family members. Indeed, family was, and still is, very important to me.

My parents led by example more than words. They never sought material gain, yet their lives were full. This is part of the legacy they passed on to their children: live life simply, but live it well. Growing up, I learned that we were not just individuals, but part of a family and a community – and as part of a community we have a responsibility to make the world we have inherited a better place for those who live beside us in the present, and for those who will come after us in the future.

My parents were quietly spoken and mild in manner. They were humble but proud people. My mother was a small woman, a great cook, and managed the house and the children. She was very handy with a needle and made a lot of our clothes. She was also quite a strong personality, with a great trust and faith in education. She wanted us girls to have proper professions because she believed that women should have the means to be independent in case they were left alone in later life. There was quite a bit of pressure put on us to succeed, for my mother wanted the best for her children and would leave no stone unturned to achieve it. She did this to a fault and if we didn't do well in an exam or get a scholarship that was up for grabs, she certainly wasn't pleased!

It was with some nervousness that I approached my mother to tell her about my decision to enter the convent. I think she was taken aback at first – but she neither encouraged, nor discouraged me; she merely warned me how strict convent life would be. Perhaps, because I was enjoying spending time with other young people – and going to parties and dances was very much a part of my life – she thought I wouldn't stick at it, and that I would soon be looking for another job. When she told my father, he was totally shocked and said nothing about it for a long time. Eventually, he simply said to my mother, 'Isn't that a damn quare thing that Treasa is doing?'

My father was tall and slim and was very much the bread-winner because he worked the farm and that was our only source of income. I never heard my parents raise their voices to each other in the house, although my mother did raise her voice to us children to sort us out when need be. And if we were fighting, we did it outside. We were never allowed to shout and scream in the house, so we took our troubles out into the garden, the yard or the shed! There was rough and tumble, and a lot of suspense in the air when there was a football match on the radio. The men would gather around and once the ball was thrown in, the next two hours were full of excitement – although no child dared speak a word until after the game had finished.

My fondest memories of home during my childhood are of Christmas time. Christmas began early in our house. It began really with baking the Christmas cake. My mother would get in a store of currants, raisins, candied peel, nutmeg and other spices, and the day of baking the cake was a big day. We gathered round the table as she mixed the ingredients, and there was a lovely aroma. When the cake went into the oven we all had to be really quiet, because we understood that if we made any noise, the cake would fall. It was very exciting, seeing the cake come out of the oven – and there was that gorgeous smell.

The other exciting Christmas preparation was the collecting of holly and ivy. We had plenty of ivy around the house and fields, but we had to go what I thought was a long distance to collect the holly. In fact it was only about half a mile away. But we had to go through the fields, because the field where the holly was was land-locked so we had to travel by foot and cross the river to get there. It was winter and the river was, I thought, very high. The smaller ones of us would have to be lifted on to somebody's back to get across it. The holly tree was not on our land. It was over in Flemmingstown. It was a beautiful tree with red berries. My father made a pile of the holly, which he bound together with a rope and brought home on his back. We carried little branches. The house was then decorated with the holly and ivy, and I thought it was lovely. And in between the holly and the ivy we would place the Christmas cards and other decorations.

Shopping was another important part of the early preparation for Christmas. Our parents went to town and brought home lots of goodies, including sweet cakes, currant cake, biscuits and sweets, and whiskey, porter and port wine. It was a tradition that the shopkeepers gave Christmas presents to their customers, and these included port wine and sherry, and different kinds of sweet cake and loaves. We shopped at Muiris Dans, Foxy Johns and Jack Connors in Dingle, and in Hicksons and Caseys in Lispole. They all gave us Christmas presents, and it wasn't about the amount they gave as much as the fact that they gave presents. We normally never had alcohol in the house, except for Christmas and for the Stations.

On Christmas Eve my parents went to town and bought whatever else was needed for Christmas. It was a day of fasting and abstinence. A tradition in the area was that on Christmas Eve we would have a fish dinner and the particular type of fish was ling. My mother would cook it when she came home from town and make white sauce with onions. We all hated fish but once that meal was over, Christmas was beginning. Another local tradition was that the whole house was lit up to welcome the child Jesus. All the windows would have a candle lit in them: even after we got electricity we still lit candles in the windows and the whole afternoon we as children spent time getting the candles ready, cutting out turnips and filling jars with sand to hold the candles. We had to wait until my father gave us the OK to light up. We couldn't wait for darkness to come! It was so exciting. The other households did the same so when we looked out towards the hillside and towards the valley, all we could see were all these little lights like lanterns hanging from the sky. That to me was magical.

On Christmas Eve night we were allowed to go to our next door neighbours, the Rourkes, to visit. Mrs Rourke was an old lady and she lived with her sons, Tom and Jack. Later on Jack married and Tom went to England. Mrs Rourke gave us lemonade, biscuits and cake and that was great, because it was a big treat at a time of rationing. We returned to our own house to get the same. My father visited the Rourkes too and he got porter and whiskey, then the neighbours Jack and Tom came to our house for the same. That would be the only visiting that would be done before

Christmas. The women stayed at home on Christmas Eve. They visited on 6 January which was small Christmas, or Nollaig na mBan (Women's Christmas), when port and Christmas cake was the usual fare.

After that visit to the neighbours was over we started to get ready for the next day. The usual washing, and getting our best clothes out. We went to bed early because we had to get up at about six in the morning to get to mass. As we went to mass in a hired car, we waited for the car to come early in the morning with great excitement. My father in the front with my brother while we all sat in the back of the car with my mother. As a child, for me one of the most thrilling things was going out in the morning, when it was still dark and the sky was full of stars, and being driven in a big fancy car.

On Christmas Day my mother put a lot of work into the dinner. Christmas Day was always a day to be at home. We never visited anyone, and were never visited by anyone that day.

The next day, St Stephen's Day, was also a great day for us as children. On St Stephen's Day, crowds of people took to the roads and streets in fancy dress, wearing masks or straw suits and accompanied by musicians, singers and dancers – remembering a festival with antecedents that long predate Christmas. It was called the Day of the Wren. They formed groups in different streets and villages, and called to each house to play and sing and dance. They were always welcomed and rewarded with donations.

The Day of the Wren, pronounced and written *wran*, was once common all over Ireland, but like many customs in rural areas it came close to extinction. From the twenties and thirties onward,

The family home in Lispole, built by my father and grandfather in 1916.

emigration took a great toll on those who would have taken part, but since the fifties there has been a revival, especially in Dingle. We loved to see the Wran, and as children we even took part in small wrans. The money raised in the collections by the big Wran went towards holding a ball in the local hotel or public house. This was a great occasion, with food and drink and craic and ceol. The party/ball was for adults only and was frowned upon by the nuns in the convent. When you returned to school after Christmas, if they heard you had been involved in the wran, you were in big trouble.

Some of the money raised was given to charity. I didn't realize as a child that I and Focus Ireland would be a beneficiary of the Wran later in life.

Our house was a two-storey farmhouse, built by my father and his father in 1916. When I was about eight years old, we got running water in the house – a little earlier than most in the area because my father was very able and, with the help of a neighbour, managed to pipe water from one of our high fields, which had a well. A few years later electricity came to the area as part of the Rural Electrification Scheme. Watching the electrician wire up the house, being able to plug a kettle into the wall socket to heat the water, or turning on the wireless by flicking a switch – this was all amazing! Yet I don't recall ever feeling deprived when we lived without these luxuries because, I suppose, everyone in the area was in the same situation.

We had a lovely garden in the front and a farmyard at the back. We had apple and other fruit trees, a small vegetable patch and lots of roses and other flowers. My mother loved her garden.

The house was situated beside a river and this river separated the parish of Lispole from Dingle. We all loved the river, and would sit on the bank and watch it flow or on the little bridge, where we spent time fishing. We'd paddle about in the shallow parts of the river, picking blackberries as we splashed about. Picking these blackberries was very important because we could sell them at the local shop and get what we thought was a substantial amount of money for them – perhaps half a crown for a bucket of blackberries.

Sometimes we fell in the river – or threw each other in – and today I am reminded of this special time when I read John O'Donohue's lines:

> I would love to live
> Like a river flows,
> Carried by the surprise
> Of its own unfolding.

When we were small, we had three bedrooms: one for my parents, one for my brother and one for the four of us girls. During my childhood, an extension was built on to the house which gave us a large kitchen and another bedroom. The kitchen was also a utility room and the hub of the house, as was the custom in those days. It was where we cooked our meals, ate and more or less lived our lives. We also had a parlour, but that was used only on special occasions and for special visits.

I date my first awareness of the spiritual from my childhood in Kerry. On summer nights, a group of us children would gather together in a field of new-mown hay. Lying on our backs, we would wait for the sky to darken and the stars to come twinkling out. We lay there enraptured by the fragrance of the hay, listening to the singing of the birds, the strange rasping cry of the corncrake from the bog, the voices of the frogs from the bog and river and the flow of the river itself. I treasure the memory of those bright summer evenings of my childhood, and I now realize – though of course I did not think of it in this way at the time – that experiences like this laid down a deep spiritual foundation.

The first time I heard the dawn chorus I was about twelve years old, and I stood at the back of the house, beside the river, where the montbretia and the fuchsia were in full bloom against mountain ash and oak trees. The glorious song of a multitude of birds broke over me, and in a moment that is still alive for me today, it was as if I had never heard birds singing before. I began to wonder if they always sang like that and I just hadn't noticed. As I stood and listened to the birds pouring out their song above me, and gazed at the beauty around me, it felt as if the day grew brighter and brighter and everything around me grew still. In fact, in those few moments, time did seem to stand still and feelings of awe and wonder took me over. I was standing in the presence of something very special, something beyond sacred.

It is very difficult to express what this experience meant to me, but when I look back at it I know it was one of the most significant moments of my life – a very special moment of awareness and mystery, for, quite suddenly, this very normal day had become extraordinary to me. And although I forgot about it for many years, I know now it was a spiritual moment too, one which drew me into a stillness that has remained with me. Right through my life, wherever I have lived, in the country or in the middle of the city, and no matter what the demands and the pressures of life, I have always sought out opportunities to experience moments of stillness, to access that special peace.

For me, nature provided the opportunity to connect with stillness, but the world of art, music or poetry can also have this effect. Even a sudden loss or an illness can bring new meaning to our lives, for we are taken out of the everyday world and our attention focuses on the other world that is always present but not always seen. A curtain is raised and we see things clearly for the first time; we know that there is another dimension to our existence.

It was not all joy, of course, back in that Kerry community where I grew up. We knew hardship through the Depression and the war, and food was rationed well into the 1950s. Hard times drove many from their land, and emigration was a curse that many local families had to learn to live with. But we were a close and neighbourly community. The local writer Peig Sayers (whom I knew as an old lady when as a child I visited her in the local hospital) put it like this:

> We all helped each other, living in the shelter of each other.
> Everything that was coming dark upon us we would disclose . . .
> Friendship is the fast root in my heart; it is like a white rose in the
> wilderness.

The community in which I grew up had a strong sense of occasion, and we took our celebrations seriously. In those days –

and this tradition still persists in some areas of the country – the people would hold religious services in their own houses. Different houses would take it in turn to hold 'the stations', as they were called, and all the neighbours would come. There would be great cleaning and decorating done in the station house in the weeks before the station, and then on the day there would be a mass held in the house, usually in the best room, and all the neighbours would gather in. Afterwards there were tea and cakes and music and dancing, and the festivities went on into the night. This tradition goes back to the Penal Laws, when the Catholic Church was suppressed, and people gathered secretly in private houses whenever a priest was available to say mass for them. In my childhood, it had become more of a community celebration, and the connection to Penal times is not often remembered.

In those days there were few cars. People walked or cycled, or travelled in pony and trap. I can remember travelling to weddings and christenings, wakes and funerals, under hedges dripping with wild fuchsia – which we called *deora Dé* (God's tears). The tradition of 'waking' the dead – maintaining an all-night vigil in the house of a person who has died – was the norm in my youth, and is still quite common in Ireland, where the rituals and traditions of death are honoured. Irish people go to funerals not just of family members and close friends but of the relations of neighbours, colleagues and acquaintances, and the expression of sympathy and solidarity at times of bereavement is very much the norm. When I was a child, we did not say that a person had died. Rather we said that they were gone *ar shlí na fírinne*, which means on the way of truth. Far from being a euphemism, this turn of phrase was an acknowledgement of death as a natural part of the cycle of life, a transition to a new phase of beauty and harmony, not an event to be feared and resented.

Monumental changes have taken place in the Church in Ireland during my lifetime. When I was growing up in Lispole, in the 1940s and 1950s, churches were full for all the masses and holy days, and there were queues for confession on Saturdays.

The annual mission, with teams of priests coming round to preach fire and brimstone, were all well attended. Lispole was a sub-parish of Dingle. There were three priests in the Dingle parish – a canon and two curates. One of the curates was assigned to Lispole, and the canon went there sometimes. The priests were among the few who drove cars – usually Morris Minors. The canon was an elderly, wiry, friendly man, and he seemed to have responsibility for the funding of the churches.

When it came to the parish dues, the canon came to Lispole and he read out the names of the subscribers in order of the size of their subscription, beginning with the highest. One year he commented on the subscriptions, being severely critical of those who in his view had not subscribed enough, according to their means. I was a young child at the time. I remember waiting and listening, with a great fear, for what he would say about us. Fortunately he said nothing, but the adults were talking and being very annoyed and angry that the canon would do such a thing in church. But on the whole, the canon was liked. One of the curates took a particular interest in sports and the development of the sports field; the other curate was very speedy in speech and otherwise, and that included giving mass. Some of the women wore shawls, and this particular curate strongly disapproved of the shawl, and spoke about it from the altar to the annoyance of the women – who continued to wear the shawls. So at the annual procession on Corpus Christi he forbade women who wore shawls to walk in the procession. Many women took offence at this, but it was the beginning of the end of shawls in Dingle.

The priests never visited the houses except for the stations and that was a very special time, when mass was said in the homes on a rota basis. In our house it came round every three and a half years. It was a huge occasion for which the houses were painted and the best wares were used: it was an occasion for a great party. One priest said mass in what was called the kitchen but was actually the sitting room, while the other heard confessions in the parlour. Everyone went to confession and communion. Outside of the stations, I thought confession was only for women and children. Children got the morning off from school; they had a big breakfast after mass and a packed lunch to take back to school to be shared with the other pupils. We all loved the stations.

In the primary school there were three lay teachers from the locality who knew all of our parents, and our parents' parents. I found school enjoyable but I knew if I wasn't smart, I would have a hard time. I also knew that it was particularly difficult for children who had learning disabilities. They were often kept at the back of the class, as if discarded. At the time there were no classes for children with intellectual or learning disabilities and I am sure they felt wronged or diminished by the treatment they received. For some reason they were branded as stupid.

Those of us who went on to secondary school went to the Presentation Convent or the Christian Brothers, both of them in Dingle. There were no lay teachers in the convent, and in general the sisters were kindly and interested in the pupils and their education.

My secondary school was in Dingle, three miles from home. Heading out the gate each day on my bike, the child was stealing out of me. Secondary school was a new world, dominated by nuns, where everything was correct and proper and one was expected to be polite, in place and on time. I did well at school. I enjoyed the camaraderie of my friends, and I was often involved in mischief and escapades. But I was lonely at times too, unhappy, rebellious, moody. I had no idea what path my life was going to take, and I was restless and unfocused. It was not until I reached school-leaving age that I began to see a way forward.

I felt, in secondary school, that the preferential treatment certain nuns gave to some children simply because they came from better-off families was wrong. One nun in particular – who was responsible for taking the fees – went out of her way to embarrass those children whose parents hadn't paid on time: she would call out their names and make them stand up in class. I thought it was very unfair and humiliating.

Other embarrassments lay ahead for those children who depended on charity for their clothes and other essential items. As the fourth girl in the family, I often had handed-down clothes from my sisters. I would have loved to have new clothes of my own but I remember feeling fortunate that at least I wasn't given other people's second-hand clothes and I felt very sad for these children.

2

A Different Path

Growing up, we had few luxuries, but we did not want for anything either. As I got older, I read that in the bigger towns and cities there were children who were poor and neglected. I wanted to help them, but I didn't know how to go about it. There were no training courses in social work in those days, and I could not think of a way to work with the poor. But I have always been a practical person, and my response was a practical one – I aimed to care for these people and help to provide for them in a most basic way.

Then I heard of an order of nuns in Dublin who worked with the poor: the Religious Sisters of Charity (often called simply the Sisters of Charity or the Irish Sisters of Charity). I did not really feel I had a vocation. I did not particularly want to be a nun, but it seemed to be the only way that I could work directly with the poor.

The Religious Sisters of Charity differ from other religious orders in one crucial respect: as well as the usual vows of poverty, chastity and obedience that all religious take when they are

With my parents after Profession, 1960.

professed as nuns or brothers, the Sisters of Charity require sisters to take a fourth vow – that of commitment to service of the poor. This difference was what attracted me to this order. That was how I stumbled into the religious life.

I entered for one reason, and remained for another: I remained because I found a deep spirituality in the Sisters of Charity, who sought to find God in all things, especially in the service of the poor and their deep faith in Divine Providence. Their trust in Divine Providence, a legacy that came directly from the foundress of the order, Mary Aikenhead, is what has sustained me in my work and throughout my life. Divine Providence is a basic belief that God will provide. It is, in essence, an act of faith. Over and over again, Mary Aikenhead talked about the 'sweet providence of a rich bank' – which meant that her trust in God was much greater than worldly goods. When her sisters needed funds, she wrote that 'the great bank on which we depend cannot fail'. Then again she says, 'We ought to have confidence in the holy bank of divine providence and allow faith to satisfy for all deficiencies of visible funds.' And, on another occasion, 'Our greatest wants with pressing necessities are nothing to our imperishable bank of his almighty providence.' Such dependence is rarely understood by the world; and less so today than ever before.

To depend on Divine Providence today is most definitely counter-cultural, but that is what we are called to as Sisters of Charity, and it is what has always sustained me in the face of difficulties. We live in a culture of achievement which believes that people should, and do, get what they deserve. But as Christians, we know that this is not so. Our activity is not based on earning our way but is more a co-operation with God to bring about a world of justice and love. Building this attitude in the culture that surrounds us requires a constant cultivation of faith.

What I didn't realize when I first entered the order was that this was God's way of calling me to walk with him and with the poor. I may not have known it at the time, but the poor were to become the inspiration for my whole spiritual development. I think often of the commitment of Jesus to the poor. In the Beatitudes he said, 'Blessed are the poor in spirit'. He didn't say, 'Blessed are those who help themselves' or 'Blessed are those who work hard and get on in life' or 'Blessed are those who try hard and succeed'. He said, 'Blessed are the poor in spirit', and his whole life shows this commitment to those who are rejected by society. He blessed people who are truculent and slow, the ones who don't turn up, the ones who 'let you down', the ones who mess things up and make a fuss, the awkward people. The poor and the poor in spirit are blessed beyond the rich and the powerful, the famous and the successful and the popular.

Over and over again, Jesus brought forward and favoured the people who are thought ill of: prostitutes, thieves, tax collectors, cripples, collaborators. And that is how, in my own way, I have tried to live my life, working with and listening to and taking into account the people that society passes by, belittles, sees as problematic and troublesome; whether I like them or don't like them, I have tried to listen to their story, see their point of view and support and champion their cause, and it has been my life as a Religious Sister of Charity that has been the bedrock of this work.

Looking back on the home in which I grew up, I can see that it was the basis of my sense of home as a place where a person can be at ease and feel free and unthreatened, and it is that sense of home that has inspired my work with homeless people. All my life, I have used myself as a benchmark when I am providing services for other people. If I could not see myself living in a place, or eating in a place, or working in a place, then I would not think it right that other people should be expected to live or eat or work there either, and that attitude underpins my thinking about the provision of services. People who are poor or sick or frail or displaced or homeless deserve the same level of comfort and ease as the rest of us. Instead of offering second-hand, substandard

My inspiration, Mary Aikenhead,
1787–1858.

conditions and services – poor services for poor people, worn-out clothes for worn-out people, cracked cups for crazed people – I have always wanted to provide high-quality goods and services for poor and marginalized people.

This way of thinking is greatly influenced by the philosophy of Mary Aikenhead (1787–1858). I knew nothing about Mary Aikenhead when I first heard about the order of nuns that she had founded, but since joining the Sisters of Charity as a young woman, I have come to know her work and her thinking, and her example is a continuing source of inspiration to me in my own life and work.

Mary Aikenhead's passionate commitment to the poor began when she heard a sermon on the story of Dives and Lazarus (Luke 16: 19–31). The picture we get in this story of Lazarus, the poor, hungry man covered with sores, is not an attractive one, but it is an accurate picture of poverty, and it was in a world of such poverty that Mary Aikenhead worked. Her focus became 'God's nobility, the suffering poor'. This is how she wrote about conditions among the poor of Dublin in her time:

It would be painful to describe the instances of heart-rending misery which we daily witness. Many in the prime of life are reduced to debility from want of food, subsisting for forty-eight hours on one meal, without sufficient clothes to cover them, their wretched furniture and tattered garments being pledged as a last resort. Within the last year we have witnessed forty cases of men willing to work, if they could procure employment, who were reduced to sickness, which in some instances terminated in death, from excessive misery.

There is no dispensary in this neighbourhood, and the poor have no other medical aid than such as we can bestow. In the course of the last summer the cholera morbus broke out ... and raged for five weeks with violence. We found some in the agonies of death, without the means even of procuring a drink ...

The lanes and streets are filled with filth ...; there are no sewers; no attention is paid to the ventilation of the houses, and the poor are obliged to buy even the water which they drink; it is of the worst description, and tends to promote disease as much by its scarcity as by its quality.

The poor are inclined to indulge in spirituous liquor; they often resort to it in despair to drown the recollection of their sufferings. The small sum which will procure spirit is insufficient to provide a meal.

The sufferings of the poor children cannot be described; many perish, and those who survive are, in many instances, so debilitated by want as to become sickly and infirm at an early period of life.

Sarah Atkinson, Mary Aikenhead: Her Life, Her Work and Her Friends, Dublin: Gill, 1875.

This is not the letter of a person removed from the experience of poverty, writing from behind a convent wall. It is the letter of a woman who clearly had a deep understanding of the circumstances and lives of the poor people in the area where she lived and a deep compassion for their suffering. What I find particularly interesting about this analysis is that she attributes the people's poverty not to their own fecklessness but to the decline of employment opportunities in the locality. With great insight, she describes how the loss of work leads directly to poverty and suffering. She recognizes the people's use of alcohol, but instead of condemning it, she explains, with compassion but without sentimentality, why it is that people who are destitute will resort to drink. For her, there was no distinction between the deserving and the undeserving poor. Her analysis was way ahead of the thinking of her time, and is radical even today.

I too had a similar experience. After three months in the novitiate I was sent out to work on a kind of placement with an older sister. Her name was Sr Agnes Eucharia, and she worked in Sandymount and Ringsend in Dublin as a parish social worker. She was a wonderful character. She had worked in England during the war and had been evacuated from her convent several times. She was a very experienced woman, and I was lucky to be sent to help her and to learn from her.

It was in October, and she was working towards Christmas. The first part of my time with her we spent begging from door to door in the Sandymount area (a well-off suburb). She had a formula: 'We are looking for your help, not for ourselves, but for families with whom we work.' We got quite a good reception, but

I found it strange and embarrassing to be begging like that. However, we collected a lot of money.

After about six weeks, we went into town to buy clothes for the poor children with the money we had gathered, and Sister Agnes bought lovely clothes, skirts and jumpers and trousers and shoes and boots and socks, much more beautiful than the clothes I had had as a child. And then she invited the families one by one up to a little centre she had, and she togged them out in these clothes. It was great to see the joy in their faces, and above all to see the respect with which she treated them. She did not want to give them second-hand clothes: she wanted them to have the best for Christmas. I saw her as living out the thinking of Mary Aikenhead in that area of Dublin. I remember her as an old lady who was respectful and determined to 'give to the poor what the rich could buy for money', as Mary Aikenhead said. She affirmed my desire to serve the poor as a Sister of Charity.

Then I was sent back to the novitiate with all its rules and regulations.

My novitiate was pre-second Vatican Council of 1962–5 and it was very strict and regulated with lots of rules to follow.

The day started at 5.30 when we got up, prayer was at 6 a.m. and mass was held at seven, after which we went to breakfast. Then, we did our manual work, which included general cleaning – sweeping, dusting, polishing the cloisters, corridors, the chapel and refectory – and that went on until 10 a.m. We then had spiritual reading for half an hour, and then it was time for lunch. After lunch we sewed, and at midday we had a fifteen-minute break for prayers. This was awareness examine: a time to give thanks, and look back and examine the day. Dinner was at 3 p.m. and was followed by recreation (which lasted for about an hour) – the only time during the day when we spoke to each other. All other activities were carried out in silence. Even our meals – except on special feast days – were taken in silence, as we listened to someone reading spiritual texts, generally the Lives of Saints.

We had evening prayer for half an hour, followed by tea and recreation. At 9 p.m. we had night prayers, again awareness examine, and then it was time for bed. Lights were put out at 10 p.m.

During the week there were also classes and spiritual exhortation, but, as you can see, the rhythm of the day was strictly determined by different activities, and the timetable we kept was intended to be a form of training in formation and timekeeping; in self-discipline and in working together in preparation for the life that was to follow – and in our vows of chastity, poverty, obedience and service to the poor.

The novitiate lasted for two and a half years. The first six months we were postulants, and during that time we spent two or three months out in other convents, working as assistants in different activities. The next year was called the spiritual year and all that time was spent in the novitiate. There was great emphasis on our spiritual formation. The following year we spent most of our time again out in ministries, learning about them and experiencing at first hand the service of the poor. It was during this period that I spent time as an assistant to a pastoral worker in the Hammersmith and Paddington area of London, where I worked with Irish families, most of them very poor. This was a real eye-opener for me because up to that point I thought people who emigrated to the UK were better off.

There is a lot to be said for some of the training during a novitiate but it certainly had its limitations. It was of its time, there was no emphasis on relationships, or human growth and development, and although we had instructions and guidance in our spiritual life, and the teachings and wisdom of Mary Aikenhead and the spirituality of St Ignatius, the founder of the Jesuits, with its focus on 'finding God in all things', no theology was taught, and there was no knowledge of or emphasis on the psychological aspects of our lives or the work we were undertaking. There was little opportunity to get to know the other novices at a personal level as we were discouraged from talking about our families or friends. Nevertheless, we formed strong friendships which lasted for years.

Admittedly, the strictness of the regime came as a shock to my youthful exuberance at first, but the companionship of the other novices, the deep spirituality of those who guided us, the serenity of some of the older sisters, the respect in which the sisters held the poor, and the prospect of working with the poor, in whom God resided in a special way, kept me going.

The name 'Stanislaus' was not my choice. I was told to take it. I knew nothing about St Stanislaus, the Polish Jesuit novice whose name is now mine. I didn't like it at first, but over time, I came to be called Stan. That is what most people call me now, and I have grown to like it.

After my novitiate, I was sent to work in a school, laundry and youth club, at Stanhope Street Convent in Dublin, in the early 1960s. In fact I now live in Stanhope Street again, in a former gate lodge to the convent, where, with others, I built and founded the Sanctuary, a spirituality centre in the heart of the city.

Back then, it was all new to me, sharing the hardship and humour of the people of Dublin and learning how to stand in solidarity with them. I loved the young people in the school and the youth club, with all their enthusiasm, vibrancy, excitement and devilment. I also loved how they were interested in helping each other and others in the community.

What I was only beginning to sense back then and I am much clearer about now is that to stand in solidarity it is not enough to sympathize with the poor or even to work to make their lives better. What is required of us is to critique the injustice that is poverty, and to understand the nature of that injustice. Poverty is not an accident of circumstance or an unfortunate but inevitable part of life. The injustice that is poverty is structural in nature – in other words, it is built into the way our society is structured and how it operates – and it can only be abolished by the dismantling of those unjust and disempowering structures.

We all live in a huge interlocking system where almost all our actions play a part in maintaining injustice. Even if we don't mean to, we are the ones who operate these unjust structures. It is not easy to disentangle ourselves from them. But we have to try to set about creating alternative structures of justice. This means putting in place procedures that promote justice. And the place to begin to do that is in our daily lives and work, as Mary Aikenhead did.

Working with and for the poor involves us in personal

relationships with poor people, and unless we enter into these relationships in the right spirit, with respect for the dignity of poor people, we are in danger of treating them with condescension or paternalism. We could even end up trying to manipulate the poor to fit in with our own plans. That is why it is so important that, in addition to trying to construct a better and more just society, we also find ways of entering into and sharing the lives of the poor.

We have a wonderful example of this in the story of Sr Catherine, a sister from Stanhope Street Convent who ministered to the sick and the dying in the workhouse in Grangegorman, County Dublin in Mary Aikenhead's time. The conditions were dreadful. As many as eight people died of cholera in one bed in one day in the workhouse. Sr Catherine worked hard for long hours, and on going home late at night, she would wash and iron lawn handkerchiefs to put on the brows of the sick and dying patients the next day. She demonstrated her respect for these destitute people by putting beautiful ironed handkerchiefs on their foreheads to try to bring them a little comfort and dignity.

Mary Aikenhead knew that there is a beauty deeply hidden in the broken bodies of the poor and of the suffering. This hidden beauty is of God. It is Jesus himself who is hidden in the poor. As he said himself, 'Whosoever welcomes one of these little ones welcomes me.' In one way it is easy to help the poor, by giving money to the appropriate organizations. But what is not easy is to stand in solidarity with the poor, to walk with them. The relationship into which the poor call us is one of deep trust, of mutual recognition, where they touch our brokenness and we touch theirs. When that happens, we are transformed. When this happens to us there is no turning back, because it is a life-changing experience. And in that transformation we find new strength – the strength of tenderness and goodness and patience and forgiveness.

When we walk with the poor, they reveal to us our hardness, our selfishness, our resistance to change. They reveal to us how imprisoned we are in our own fears. They teach us not to turn aside from our pain, or anguish or brokenness or emptiness by pretending to be strong. They teach us to go into ourselves, to go down the ladder of our own being until we discover in our vulnerability the shining light in the darkness, the presence of Christ.

When we walk with the poor, we have to learn not to be surprised if they reject us. They have suffered a great deal at the hands of the knowledgeable and the powerful. These are not the people the poor need and want. What they want are people who will respect them. Often we must simply suffer with the poor, at times having nothing to offer but our presence, being with and standing with them.

Mary Aikenhead knew there was something very fragile in the poor and that if we are not careful, we can walk on it, crush it, ignore it or pass it by. She knew that when Jesus was speaking with the Samaritan woman, he was not just speaking to the poor of the world: he was speaking to the poor in each of us, the broken part of our being, where there is so much fear and where we have no belief in our ability to love and be loved. Mary Aikenhead knew that to stand in solidarity with the poor is not to give of our riches but to reveal to the poor their own riches, their value, their gifts and to trust them and their capacity to grow.

3

A Turn in the Road

My life took an unexpected turn when a young bishop, Peter Birch, was appointed to the Diocese of Ossory, in Kilkenny in the mid-1960s, just around the time of the Vatican Council, which brought with it a great sense of renewal in the Church. In those days, social services were practically non-existent in Ireland, and Bishop Birch's work in setting up Kilkenny Social Services was pioneering.

This was the sort of work I was longing to do, but, as it happened, it wasn't I who made the decision. Bishop Birch was looking for someone to help in his work, and my order sent me to join him. When I arrived in Kilkenny, the bishop was away. He had been called to Rome, to the Vatican Council, so when I started in Kilkenny I was sent first to work with another two Sisters of Charity, Sr Mary Campion Heavey and Sr Jude Cullinan. It was in fact Sr Campion who first approached Bishop Birch about social services in the diocese. She had studied social science at University College Dublin (UCD), and had also worked in

My mentor and good friend, Bishop Peter Birch.

different parts of the country. Experience in the USA and Britain made her keenly aware of the changes which were taking place abroad.

Everything was very primitive in the centre in Kilkenny. We had a small office with just a little desk, a table really, and one proper chair at the desk. The other chairs were seats from a motor car.

Sitting in this office one day, I looked out the window and saw the bishop getting out of his car. I was on my own at the centre. I took fright – I had never met a bishop before; I'd never even seen one, except at confirmation – and I ran out the back door and left the place empty! Of course when I came to my senses, I had to go back to the office. I couldn't leave the bishop there all alone. When I got back, he was laughing at me. He knew how nervous I was. As it turned out, he was very easy to get on with and to work with. In fact, he was a humble, shy man, and I found it easy to relate to him. I was excited about his programme of care, and like many in Kilkenny at the time, I responded to it; and because I believed in it, I wasn't daunted by it. Although it was an exhilarating time, it was very hard work too. During my first year my main duty focused on home help. For example, one old man I attended, Dan, needed help in getting up, getting dressed, lighting a fire and generally keeping his home clean and tidy. Although during the day Dan received meals on wheels and had visitors, every evening I would return to his house to make his tea and ensure that he was safe and comfortable.

Another duty of mine was to cook for a family. The mother suffered from post-natal depression and her baby was cared for by her sister. I cooked for the rest of the family – the four children who remained at home, and their father, who bought ingredients for me to prepare the meals. On one occasion, he'd bought some minced meat and I hadn't a clue what to do with it. I raced back to the convent on my bike, took instructions on how to cook the mince and then cycled back to the house as fast as I could to prepare the meal for the family. I felt more than a little foolish!

After Sister Campion and Sister Jude left, I stayed on and in the end I was there for twenty years, except that I went away to study, first at UCD, where I did a degree in Social Science, and afterwards to Manchester to do postgraduate work.

Bishop Birch was an outspoken advocate for a comprehensive programme of community care and social services, but most people in Ireland in the early 1960s didn't even know what terms like 'community care' and 'social services' meant. Britain's welfare state was already well established, but in Ireland supports for people with social needs were very underdeveloped. There were no allowances for single parents, for example, or the dependants of prisoners. People in need of care were expected to be looked after in institutions.

Statutory community-based personal social services were largely non-existent. The universities were only beginning to develop the training of social workers, and there were only a handful of professional social workers in the whole of Ireland, who were generally employed by hospitals. It wasn't until the mid-1970s, after the eight regional health boards were established, that the community care programme developed and we saw the beginning of community-based social services in Ireland – and social workers being employed by the state.

There were of course charities, many of them church-related, doing various kinds of work with people in need, but their work was piecemeal and uncoordinated. All this was to change, but when I first worked in Kilkenny, these ideas were only starting to develop.

Ireland was a very poor country in the 1930s, '40s and '50s, with no official social or economic policies. It wasn't until 1958 that the first clearly stated economic policy was published in the Whitaker Report. Apart from income maintenance for the old, the unemployed and widows, and the work undertaken by charities, there was little else for the poor and underprivileged in the community.

When I began working with Bishop Birch in the early 1960s, living standards in Ireland were still low and emigration and unemployment rates were extremely high. The country was in the doldrums. However, there was some hope ahead because of the Whitaker Report and because government thinking, under the Taoiseach Sean Lemass, was beginning to change, and new programmes of economic expansion were set in motion. Business and industry were starting to come into their own, emigration began to decline, and the educational system was radically improved and modernized, first at primary level and then at second and third levels. With the advent and spread of television came growing participation in debate and controversy on social, moral and religious issues, encouraging a much more questioning social outlook and receptiveness to change on the part of the public. People began to be aware of and demand their constitutional rights, and alongside this came the growth of special interest groups, which had not existed in the 1950s. The civil rights movement in America influenced thinking in Ireland, and the women's movement began to influence Irish thinking too.

Enormous psychological change had occurred in Ireland. The conviction that things could be improved dawned on a people hitherto conditioned to believe that they could only get worse. And at the centre of this growing conviction, in the Kilkenny area, was the uncomfortable prophetic activism of Peter Birch.

Treading new ground, Bishop Birch set out to build and develop what he called the Local Church, where bishops and clergy would no longer 'lord' it over people, but would be servants of the people and God, where the dignity of every human being was respected, and where people would genuinely care for each other, look out for each other in the best Christian sense. The people who, in the past, were on the margins of society were now to be given a special place, and recognized not only for their needs, but for the contribution they could make to society. This was a huge change. It turned the current thinking upside down. It challenged everyone to rethink the values they lived by and aspired to. For me too, this was a very different way of thinking from what I'd been used to. It was something I had to work through for myself and try to absorb. It was something that I had to be prepared to live and work by: what was central was the inherent dignity of every individual and their right to be able to live out their life with dignity – no matter what their social status.

While this new thinking was very exciting and persuasive, it was also very challenging. And not everybody agreed with it. At times, people challenged it and they would disagree with me and my views. Having to take a different position when faced with people who were much older than me was difficult. And it meant, at times, that being unpopular was part of the price that had to be paid for following this new thinking.

But inspired by the bishop, I worked, prayed, struggled and suffered for this ideal. Influenced by the liberation theology coming from South America and a new wave of radical thinking in the Church and society, together we were constantly discovering new ideas, ways, images and visions – new needs, new services, new experiments. The young and the old, the rich and the poor, the able and the disabled, the sick and the well, the learned and the unlearned, the homed and the unhomed all had a place and a gift. Bringing the periphery into the centre, creating services, activities and communities, touching the hearts of rich and poor alike, consoling the poor and disquieting the rich with the good news of the Gospel, we set out to build a new style of church, vibrant, exciting, always changing, renewing, seeking, listening, reading, waiting, speaking, campaigning, never satisfied. We invited new ideas, thoughts and people from   onstant stream of priests, poets, artists, thinkers, campaigners, prophets and saints converged on the small city of Kilkenny from all over the world, and we in turn went to see communities and projects all over the world. Many of the people we met and learned from and worked with in those years became our friends for life.

Bishop Birch came from an academic background – he had

been Professor of Education at Maynooth College, the National Seminary for Ireland, and was a very learned man – and he had a lot of respect for academic institutions. He developed very strong links – with both professors and students – with UCD in particular, especially the Department of Social Science. The teaching staff of the college often came to Kilkenny to hear what we were doing, and provided a theoretical and reflective input.

This was also new: people were not used to linking the theoretical framework to the practical.

There was a constant exchange between the university and Kilkenny Social Services, which was seen by the university as a new model of care. Particularly interesting to the teaching staff was the finding of placements for students – and for us on the ground it was an inspiring learning experience.

But although an academic, Bishop Birch was deeply concerned about people and their problems. This concern underlay his commitment to the provision of services. He had great insight and imagination and a wealth of contacts, and these powered his ability to get the best specialist advice on social problems and how to address them. Yet despite his concern for people, he was not an extrovert and he did not enjoy social occasions; he could even come across as rather grim. But he was a great 'ideas man' and he knew how to get people's interest and inspire them.

One way he had of disseminating his ideas was to hold informal meetings with small groups of friends, together with some of the local priests. Sr Campion helped to form these groups with Bishop Birch. She provided an analytical background and had a very large input in that first year. All this happened before I arrived in Kilkenny.

No records of those meetings were kept, but even people who did not fully share the bishop's vision of social caring found that they were committing themselves to helping him, either out of friendship or because they felt sorry for him. What seems to have happened at those meetings is that idealism and pragmatism met, laying a solid foundation on which the later organization was established.

In 1963, Bishop Birch addressed an open meeting of between a hundred and a hundred and fifty in Kilkenny. This was the inaugural meeting of the Kilkenny Social Services, and included priests, nuns, doctors, nurses and representatives both of the local authority and of voluntary bodies. The bishop outlined what he wanted: a comprehensive programme of community care incorporating the various groups connected with social services, both statutory and voluntary. The enormous breadth of Bishop Birch's plans was also indicated. He made clear his determination to see that no aspect of underprivilege should be left unattended.

It would be inaccurate to say that there were no services whatsoever in the area before the foundation of Kilkenny Social Services. There were in fact several voluntary organizations, many of them church-based (such as the Society of St Vincent de Paul and the Legion of Mary) and the Ladies Association of Charity doing work of different kinds in the area.

What was revolutionary about Bishop Birch's approach was how he brought all these volunteers and activists together and coordinated the work so that it was much more effective. When his social services centre was up and running, people could be referred to the centre or choose to come themselves. Each case could be assessed, and the most appropriate responses identified, and the person's needs would be met, at least partially, whereas in the past, what assistance was available was more hit and miss.

That first public meeting created enormous interest and some offers of practical help and equipment followed. A businessman gave us premises in the centre of the city, a local doctor offered a washing machine, and the Society of St Vincent de Paul quickly offered three more when it became obvious that there was a need for a launderette for old people. So we opened a launderette, which was staffed by volunteers. Schoolchildren collected clothes for washing, and after local women had washed, dried and ironed them, the children returned the freshly laundered clothes.

Bishop Birch was very aware of the needs of old people. At that time, there were no meals on wheels, for example; and nothing to support old people living alone. There was a kind of assumption that if someone had been looking after themselves and cooking for themselves all their lives, there was no reason why they should need help with these things as they got older. Bishop Birch's way of tackling this issue was to get people in from the outside, from other countries in Europe or the States or wherever, to talk about what they were doing. We got a lady from Amsterdam. Miss Boss was her name and she was rather bossy too, but she gave talks about what they were doing to provide services for the aged in Holland. People, including those from voluntary bodies and local authorities, doctors, nurses, priests and nuns – and members of the public – listened and were interested, but they were still dubious about it, so we just went ahead and started to provide meals for a small number of old people. By degrees people began to see the value of the work, and they started to ask for the services in their areas.

That was the way the bishop worked. Instead of trying to convince people that there was a problem, he would show them a solution, and suddenly they would see that there had been a problem all along and would get enthusiastic about the solution. This is also true of the way people think about social issues. If you draw their attention to poverty, they will often say that some people are poor because they are lazy or because they are protected by social welfare, but if, instead of trying to change their minds by argument, you show them a way forward that could make things better for poor people, they will often see the point and will agree with the solution, even if they had not hitherto acknowledged that there was a problem at all. So Bishop Birch could implement social change very quickly because he was able to bring people with him. The insight into how to get people to work with you by leading them to perceive solutions rather than problems is something that I learned from the bishop and it has been a basic method in my own work all these years.

Within a few weeks of that first meeting in Kilkenny, teams were formed to cook meals, to work on the befriending service for young mothers with large families and to clean and redecorate where necessary. Virtually all the work was done on a voluntary basis. For example, the meals-on-wheels women cooked meals in their own homes and delivered them to older people and others in need, and they did this on a rota system. Little money was spent, but within the first year a fund-raising committee was established, which helped greatly.

So much energy had already been harnessed by various projects that there was simply no stopping it. Premises for a children's play-centre were offered and volunteers came to work in the launderette.

Local religious – men and women from practically all the orders in Kilkenny – offered to help other voluntary organizations with the cleaning, decorating and continued maintenance of the old almshouses which housed the elderly and were in a poor state of repair. And there were many other people who registered their willingness to take on any voluntary work offered them or required of them.

Outside experts were invited to the second public meeting in Kilkenny, and dozens of needs were identified by the people who attended. Not everyone agreed with the bishop. Some preferred not to rock the boat, and some didn't like the bishop's very direct approach, but there was nevertheless a groundswell of support for the work, and useful outlets were identified for the energy and concern aroused by the meetings and by the bishop's ideas. People laughed at some of his suggestions at first, but these same people found themselves volunteering to help out on schemes that they had initially thought plain daft or unworkable. The bishop created a kind of stunned willingness among potential volunteers to go along with most of his ideas. One volunteer said she agreed to something he asked her to do because the idea of being asked to do something by a bishop was just so unusual, she couldn't say no. He came up with all sorts of ways of helping people, and he was the first person to suggest free meals for all schoolchildren, an idea that was not well received, and is still not widely implemented, even in schools in the poorest areas. He noticed that there were fewer people availing themselves of third-level education in Kilkenny than in other counties, so he came up with the idea of getting a bus so that students could go to university in Dublin and come back in one day. He thought this would be an encouragement for them, but his suggestion was just laughed at. Only today are people starting to think of doing this.

Bishop Birch also supported the establishment of home crafts to give women an independent income. Although this was a small enterprise, where we helped women with knitting and sewing of items and crafts that could be sold in shops and town centres, it was an important initiative in providing women with some independence.

Bishop Birch really stirred it up when it came to the Travellers. Again, in the 1960s, Travellers were hardly talked about, but the bishop thought about them. I remember one Sunday he came up to me and said he was thinking of going to a man who made caravans, out in a rural part of Kilkenny, to ask him for one. I thought he meant he was looking for a caravan for a Travelling family. But no, his idea was that a group of us should go out and live with the Travellers for a while and get to know them, build up trust. Not that we should learn to trust the Travellers, but that they should learn to trust us. Bishop Birch liked the Travellers very much. He came from a rural background himself, and he enjoyed talking to them and hearing their stories.

I went along with him to get the caravan and then people went out and lived on a Travellers' caravan site. We all did it in our turn. It was a brilliant idea, for it was such a good way to make contact with the Travellers. But people thought it was the craziest thing they had ever heard. Of all the crazy things he did, this was really considered the craziest. But that's how he was. If he thought it was right, he went for it and he did it.

When Bishop Birch's ideas on the provision of social services failed, it was often because he was ahead of his time, and people were not yet receptive to what he was proposing. Yet what Dr Birch himself called 'some of the dafter-looking ideas' paid off handsomely.

Bishop Birch's socially innovative work had its foundations, of course, in his Christian faith. Bishop Harry Murphy of Limerick was also becoming interested in the provision of social services and was a close friend of Bishop Birch's, and together they attended the Vatican Council. The first recognition of the work they were doing back in Ireland came from the council, when they learned that bishops from other countries were talking and thinking and acting about poverty in the same way.

As a way of integrating the work in the social services with the life of faith, Bishop Birch introduced the cursillo. This is a weekend in which people come together to express their Christianity and solidarity, enabling them to understand their faith better and their responsibility and obligations to themselves and their neighbour as committed Christians. It is an attempt to help people to integrate their life of work and prayer and charity, and almost everyone involved in the social services attended a cursillo weekend. The cursillo was a retreat that was directed by laypeople. It is a movement that came from South

America, and it was very much in keeping with the spirit of the Kilkenny Social Services. It provided a spiritual dimension to the work, and the most significant thing about it was that up to then all retreats were directed by priests. This was a movement which included priests and nuns – but the direction of it was by laypeople.

The Birch experiment worked so well because the bishop's ideas appealed to people, and it allowed everyone to get involved and to take ownership of the movement. The availability of sisters of different religious communities to work in the social services was also significant. They did not have to be paid, and as nuns they were accepted in the community. And not only were they nuns, but they were professionally qualified in social work or nursing.

Bishop Birch was totally committed to the poor and he had a very good understanding of people on the margins. He had a brother with Down's syndrome, and that close personal experience made him sensitive to the needs of people with learning disabilities. At that time, mental handicap (the term in use in those days) was almost a taboo subject. It was certainly hidden and hardly spoken about, and the services for people with intellectual disabilities were very underdeveloped. Having watched his own brother growing up, Bishop Birch was very aware of the kinds of services that were needed in this area. Four social science students were assigned to work in Kilkenny in the summer of 1964, and one of those students later carried out a survey of mentally handicapped children in the diocese; this study formed the basis of our planning for schools.

In fact, a school for learning-disabled children called Mother of Fair Love was one of the first services set up. It was a very creative and progressive school, and continues to be so. Hostels followed, and later a workshop for mentally handicapped adults. The workshop the bishop set up on the Callan Road on the outskirts of the city – which is still there – was a model. This is known as SOS, which stands for Special Occupation Scheme. It wasn't your average sheltered workshop, with people doing mundane and repetitive tasks. There was silk screening, pottery, gardening, all very innovative and inspiring. At that time the Kilkenny Design Centre was active, and we got them involved too. The Design Centre would provide the designs and the people in the workshop would carry out the work. So we were making a link between some of the most highly respected people in the community and people who had been regarded as having no intelligence, as having made no contribution to society. Everything was beautifully done. There was nothing shoddy – it would have been impossible for the bishop to accept that.

At that time – it's hard to believe it now – mentally handicapped people weren't allowed to receive Holy Communion because they weren't seen to have reached 'the age of reason'. Bishop Birch constantly said that this was nonsense, that these are human beings, if just a bit slow. People were outraged at the idea that they should be given communion, but in the end he started simply to administer it himself, and he got priests in the diocese to do it too. That was the kind of leader he was.

In a very short time we had created a whole range of services in the diocese for people with mental handicaps, for preschool children – playgroups before playgroups had even been heard of in the rest of the country – for older people, for families. We set up family resource centres, for example. This is still thought of as a new idea in Ireland, but we had them back then, lots of groups for mothers, parenting groups and so on. Having established schools for people with intellectual disabilities, Bishop Birch then identified the needs of children who were intelligent but who couldn't participate in class for various reasons – they might have been a bit disturbed, for example – and he set up a small school for these children. There were only eight children in it, and it was a lovely school. That kind of service still doesn't exist in other parts of Ireland.

Other notions worked because of their simple practicality. The Ways and Means Committee, for example, was basically a fund-raising and financial committee made up of businessmen who knew how to make money and how to spend and invest it. The finances were left totally in their hands.

One of their initiatives was a weekly raffle, known as the Kilkenny Draw. It was called Puss Club, after the Kilkenny Cats. What made it attractive was that it provided cash prizes – the first prize being £100 (a lot of money in those days) – and it attracted almost as much attention in Kilkenny as the national lottery does in Ireland today. The raffle was carried out in a ceremonious and public manner and caused great excitement. We need to see this raffle in the context of the poverty of that era and the absence of ready cash – and we need to realize that it was the main source of income for social services at that time!

The first few years of Kilkenny Social Services were heady

days, and we achieved a great deal, but it wasn't really until the early 1970s that we were in a position to do more than respond to emerging needs, to assess the situation and plan the development of our services.

Bishop Birch was always a great believer in the principle of learning what is useful from the next parish, diocese, country or continent, and that was part of the reason we had so many people coming to visit us from all over the world. They helped not only in the development of the organization but also in shaping it. The bishop also put a lot of emphasis on excellence. When establishing a new social project, he would seek excellent specialist advice – what is now known as 'best practice' – at both national and international levels, and this commitment to high standards was behind the stream of visitors who came to Kilkenny to talk to us and advise us on what we were about. We all learned from them, and we went to visit them in Sweden, Holland, France, Australia, America, Scotland and other parts of Britain, to learn and bring back ideas.

At the same time, Bishop Birch valued the contribution of volunteers. 'We cannot,' he said, 'leave all the healing to specialized professional people. We're all called to be healers. In fact, specialists can only retain their humanity if they see their specialization as a form of service they carry out as part of and not instead of the people of God.'

A lesson I found hard to learn was that being professional and efficient wasn't everything. I would go away to train and when I came back I had all these wonderful professional ideas, and would want to get things moving and more efficient, but

Bishop Birch would say that to retain humanity in a service, it must move not at the pace of the efficient ones but at the pace of those who move more slowly and take time to get things done. He said that over and over and over again and it was a very good lesson for me. Later, when I went to different countries on fellowships – to the States and all over Europe – looking at services, the thing that struck me was that while some of the services were very professional and efficient, they were also clinical and cold, which was exactly what the bishop had said would happen if services became too professional. In his work Bishop Birch tried to combine the professional with the voluntary. We had hundreds of volunteers all over the diocese. There were centres in each parish where people worked, both professionals and volunteers. That combination led to a more humane service, but it is hard to maintain. He managed to maintain it, however, by constantly encouraging both. By talking to people, especially volunteers, he would keep in touch with what was going on and what the real needs were on the ground. I have tried to retain that model, mixing volunteers with professionals. The most striking thing about Bishop Birch, in my view, was his inclusiveness. For example, when Cardinal William Conway, just after his appointment as Primate of All Ireland, was invited to Kilkenny to open the Social Studies Summer School, the bishop suggested that the newly formed girls' youth club from the poorest part of the town, which I was involved in, should put on a drill display for the occasion. The day centred around a garden party to which both the well-off and the beneficiaries of the social services were invited. The display was to be the only entertainment – a prospect which dismayed many, who expected it to be an ostentatious flop. In fact, largely because it was so unusual, the idea worked beautifully and the occasion was a huge success. The girls and the spectators learned something about self-reliance and autonomy.

Another example of his inclusiveness was the way Bishop Birch involved laypeople in his work; this may sound rather obvious, but it is surprising how firmly the Church excludes the laity. I attended the funeral in Kilkenny in 2010 of the woman who had been Bishop Birch's secretary from the very beginning. She was the first layperson in the country ever appointed as secretary to a Roman Catholic bishop, and as far as I know, at her death more than forty years later, she was still the only laywoman who had ever served in this capacity in Ireland – an indication of a narrowness of attitude in the Church in general and of the forward-looking thinking of Bishop Birch all those years ago. I often think that if more bishops had been like him and the Church had been open to working in conjunction with laypeople, we might not be in the mess we are in today with a Church in dire straits and fast losing touch with its people.

The Church has always been inward-looking, and a celibate and hierarchical clergy supports that inwardness. It isn't just that the laity are neglected or forgotten: especially in those days, they were deliberately excluded from the work of the Church. As religious, we were instructed to keep a distance between ourselves and laypeople and, frankly, not to trust them. I remember a small but telling incident from my days as a young nun. We used to eat in a refectory next to a kitchen where laypeople worked. There was a door between the kitchen and the dining areas, and one day I left the door open. I was roundly reprimanded for this, because it meant that the ordinary people could see the nuns eating – a shocking level of familiarity!

This distrust of the laity still permeates the Church's thinking, and is at the root of the appalling lack of respect for the civil law that the Church has shown in the matter of the non-reporting of the sexual abuse of children by members of the clergy.

Working with the laity is a profound requirement for the Church if it is to grow and prosper. Back then, when I first went to work with him, Bishop Birch was already seen as different. He had an understanding of the lives of ordinary people that is most unusual among a celibate clergy with limited experience of family life.

Before he was made Bishop of Ossory, when he was still a professor in Maynooth, Bishop Birch was involved in working with prostitutes in Dublin. He saw prostitutes as victims. In the course of that work, he discovered that many of them had grown up in institutions, and that made him interested in institutional care. He wanted to make life in institutions better, to change things for the children. He wanted the boys and girls to be brought up together, which was considered a revolutionary idea, and he wanted both men and women to be in charge of children's homes. In the 1960s, he suggested that boys in St Patrick's Boys' Residential School, run by my own order, the Religious Sisters of Charity, should move into St Joseph's Girls' Residential School, which was run by the same order, thus leaving St Patrick's free for moderately and severely handicapped children. This was an unusual notion at the time, but the transfer was carried out successfully over a period of three years. He campaigned a lot nationally in the area of childcare, and if he had lived and had had a chance to effect that kind of reform in residential institutions, the terrible things that went on in care might have been revealed earlier and a stop put to them.

Partly because of this interest in residential care, that became one of the areas of reform in Kilkenny. In 1970 we set up the first professional course in the country for people involved in childcare. This course, leading to a Diploma in Residential Child Care, provided training and education for twenty students from all over Ireland each year for the following ten years. This was a major new development, because up to that point there was no professional training for residential childcare workers in Ireland.

All my life I have retained an interest in this area, and just as Bishop Birch saw how institutional life was linked to prostitution, I could see why so many young people who become homeless had spent all or part of their childhood in institutional care. Again, setting up the childcare course was an innovative move, for at the time childcare was considered the responsibility of the Church, and here we were opening up training possibilities to laypeople.

Kilkenny Social Services became a template for the future development of voluntary community services and was widely admired. Largely as a result of the thinking coming out of Kilkenny, the government established the National Social Service Board in 1974. Erskine Childers, the Minister for Health at the

The Board and some of the staff from Kilkenny Social Services.

time, appointed three social workers as ambassadors, to move around Ireland to establish voluntary social services. When he was establishing the new health boards in 1970, he ensured that there was representation of the voluntary sector on each board, and in fact I myself was appointed to the first South-Eastern Health Board by Erskine Childers.

All through the time that I worked in Kilkenny (from the 1960s to the early 1980s) I lived in a convent that shared a campus with

St Joseph's: it was what was called in those days an industrial school, where boys and girls who could not remain in their own home, for different reasons, were placed in care. St Joseph's was run by my own order, by nuns that I knew, and every day on my way to work I would pass by it and see the children coming and going. It later emerged that horrific sexual and physical abuse of the boys was taking place in this school at the hands of two men who were employed there, throughout the years that I lived as the school's neighbour.

This revelation, in 1995, came as a profound shock, and I was horrified by what had been done to the children – and by the realization that it had been going on practically under my nose. I also felt ashamed and desperately sorry and sad that it took place in a residential home run by the Sisters of Charity, my own order. I can well understand that people find it hard to believe that someone living so close to such horrors had no inkling of what was going on. I find it hard to understand myself. At a recent reunion of those who studied on the Residential Child Care Course in Kilkenny, I talked to some of my own former students about this. They too had been very shocked by the revelations, and were astounded to think that they – who were after all professionally interested in the welfare of children in care, some of whom had worked on placement in St Joseph's – had been unaware of what was happening practically next door to them. It is an indication of how dark and hidden these abusive acts are, how frightened the children were, and the gulf that existed between adults, even caring adults, and the children they were responsible for.

The media have done us all an important service in bringing

child abuse in institutions to light and exposing both the perpetrators and those who covered up for them. Without the initial work of investigative journalists, the Ryan inquiry would probably never have been undertaken. (Its official report on abuse in religious-run institutions for children commissioned by government was published in 2009.) I have myself been accused of complicity in the St Joseph's case, and I try to put this horrible experience into perspective beside the dreadful pain inflicted on those young boys. Still, it would be dishonest of me not to admit that I have found the accusations deeply wounding, and I am still working to recover from the effect they have had on me.

Bishop Birch was a social entrepreneur, I suppose, the kind of person who takes risks, who asks the right questions and is able to live with the unanswered questions and let other questions emerge and let the questions become the answers and still be able to stay with the process. He was stubbornly committed to his work yet was always open to change and he always remained faithful to the beliefs. That's my idea of a social entrepreneur. It's like any entrepreneur, really. You have to be like that if you want to keep ahead of the posse, and that was how he was by nature, those were the gifts he had.

It was from Bishop Birch that I learned about speaking in public. He would always take even the smallest opportunity to speak and say something worthwhile. He might simply be open-ing an exhibition or speaking to a small group of volunteers, maybe saying only a few words, but he always used the oppor-tunity to say something of significance that people would remember. I have always kept this in mind, and I try to use my opportunities in a similar way, to make a real contribution.

I prepare well for my talks, and in the early days I would practise giving my talks out loud while driving my car. Once I felt ready, I was confident to go ahead in public. My confidence also came from the fact that I really believed in the message I was conveying – and believed in what I was doing. So it was belief, preparation and practice that helped me to stand up in public and speak.

I wonder what Bishop Birch would do today, what he would say about how society is becoming so fragmented, the lack of trust in the political system, the social system, the religious system, the Church, the judiciary – all of these institutions. I do believe he saw it coming, and if he were here today, he would be one of the people expressing an alternative view. He said to me not long before he died that there would be no religious orders in the future, so we should bring together laypeople who want to live as a community, maybe for a short or long time, and be of service. Whether people are attached to a religious institution or not doesn't matter, he said. He thought that was one way of maintaining services and a commitment to the poor and to those on the margins. This was as far back as the 1970s. He saw the fragmentation coming, and he was thinking through how we might put things in place to give people hope; and at the same time was planning how we could constantly challenge the system to make sure it changes.

What Bishop Birch left me with was a deep desire to see things through to their completion and to see the possibility in people and in situations. In Bishop Birch's eyes, everybody was an artist of some kind and it is up to us to try to help them to realize their potential, to try to identify people's particular gifts and skills and to draw them out. He was committed to establishing social services, but he also wanted everyone to experience valuable things, things that would be healing and that would bring beauty into their lives.

4

Combating Poverty

As well as being an activist and a social pioneer, Bishop Birch was a thinker and a very influential speaker. He spoke out against injustice. At a very early stage he spoke against physical punishment in schools and against capital punishment (both of which existed in Ireland back then), and in favour of civil divorce. Although he believed that marriage was for life and he would protect that bond whenever he could, he also believed that divorce was a civil right. Divorce was then not only illegal in Ireland but unconstitutional, so he drew down the wrath of priests and other bishops, and indeed laypeople too. He attracted the more progressive, and people who were seeking out new things, and got a lot of criticism from the conservative majority. But it was always the issue of poverty and social justice that most exercised him, and the Christian concern for justice articulated by Bishop Birch was and remains the driving force in my own search for justice and solutions to the difficulties of people on the margins of society.

In 1971, the Catholic Bishops' Conference's Committee on

Chatting with the late Dr Garret FitzGerald at the Poverty Conference
in Kilkenny, 1971. (Photo by Derek Speirs)

Social Welfare held a conference in Kilkenny. This conference on
poverty stirred up a national debate, for the issue until then had
not been faced up to in Ireland. Bishop Birch was a key speaker at
this watershed conference. He spoke about the Christian's
obligation to transform society, change the structures and social
and economic policies which interfered with the freedom of man.
A social worker told him, after the address, that he was 'preaching
socialism'. Bishop Birch replied, echoing Cardinal Manning's
remark of a century earlier, that to him it was 'plain Christianity'.

To establish a Christian social service was not an easy matter.
Certain myths had to be attacked. At this conference I presented a

paper on poverty and the Church. I urged the leadership of the Church to identify with the poor and to challenge the status quo. I didn't think there was anything very controversial in what I said; I only gathered together the ideas I heard being discussed all around me. I was not to know that what people might say privately and among activists was not considered acceptable by many, either church people or the public in general. So I was very surprised when I got into big trouble about what I had said. My order took a dim view, and I was told that I was not to speak publicly again on social issues.

I took a very old nun's advice. She said, 'Just stay quiet for a while – six months or so – and then slowly and gently start to speak out again. Don't ask for permission because you won't get it!' That was exactly what I did.

What I found most upsetting and frustrating at this time was that I didn't believe I was being very radical. In some ways, I was only saying in public what some were saying or thinking in private. I also regarded it as part of my work. I was involved in the service of the poor, and bringing about justice – and it all seemed so very natural to me. But very quickly I discovered that when you are in the public eye, people either agree or disagree with you. They admire you or resent you – love you or hate you. I discovered this at an early stage and it was difficult to accept that it was part and parcel of the life. In fairness, I think that the order had no experience of one of its sisters being in the public eye. The order was used to working quietly with no strong opinions expressed and no publicity. But in my view there was no conflict as long as I worked and spoke with integrity, and it did not go to my head, or I lost the run of myself.

Speaking at the launch of the Annual Report of the National Committee on
Pilot Schemes to Combat Poverty, 1978. (Photo by Derek Speirs)

In fact I was always getting into big trouble right through the 1970s and into the late 1980s for expressing my views on social issues. The problem I had was that I really believed I was carrying out the work that I was meant to do and that it was in keeping with the spirit of Mary Aikenhead, and with the spirit of the documents from the Second Vatican Council. I wouldn't say I was rebellious. I think a lot of the uneasiness in my order came from a distrust of the media, and any publicity was seen as problematic. But by the late 1980s and early 1990s, the Religious Sisters of Charity had changed their attitude, and since then have been very supportive of my work. Without their support at that time, both moral and financial, I would not have been able to do many of the things I have done in my life as a campaigner and activist and as a provider of services. But back in the old days, the sisters were inclined to toe the line, and they expected me to do so too – an expectation that I frequently challenged.

Bishop Birch supported me through the earlier, difficult time, and I have always been grateful to him for that. He challenged people to think about their own attitudes. He asked them if they were living a simple life according to what Jesus himself laid down as appropriate for Christians. Those questions made people uneasy and opposition to our views about social justice became more muted.

But the paper that really made the headlines from that conference was given by Séamus Ó Cinnéide. In it he made the startling assertion that a quarter of the population was living in poverty, a revelation that fired the public social conscience and public outrage in about equal measure.

The way of thinking that emerged from the Kilkenny

Conference on Poverty was new and very much in contrast to the way Irish society viewed social issues at the time. Labour Party activists were strongly influenced by the conference, and when Labour came to power as part of a coalition government in 1973, the elimination of poverty was articulated for the first time as a priority for government. The European Community Programme to Combat Poverty was initiated in 1975 (largely due to the efforts of Frank Cluskey, later leader of the Irish Labour Party). When the Irish government established the Committee on Pilot Schemes to Combat Poverty to co-ordinate the work of this programme in Ireland, I was appointed chair.

This programme was radical in its thinking, since it defined poverty in structural terms and perceived that the elimination of poverty required the redistribution of resources in society. It highlighted the importance of including people who are excluded and piloted new approaches to action-research which combined research, action, advocacy and policy. It had a strong focus on community development and empowerment. It helped people to set up co-operatives in rural areas and, in urban areas, it supported the development of resource centres and began structured welfare rights work. The programme supported projects on disability, women and violence and the Traveller community.

However, the forces of conservatism hadn't gone away, and when the coalition government was defeated in 1977, commitment to combating poverty faltered. The Minister for Health at the time, Charles Haughey, asked me a number of times if I understood the consequences of speaking out against government policy. He would remind me that our work was funded by the government and told me my job was to 'serve the poor', not to campaign.

The conclusion of the Combat Poverty Report on Poverty published in 1980 was that poverty was due to structural inequalities within Irish society. This analysis was not accepted by the government of the day – Haughey was by now Taoiseach (Prime Minister) – and the Report was effectively stifled and revised. In that same year, coincidentally or otherwise, the government stopped funding for our crucial projects. I cannot say definitively that the decision to stop funding those projects was a deliberate payback for public criticism, but that is certainly my perception. Attempts to stifle the voices of those who advocate on behalf of the voiceless in our community are not new, of course; nor are they unique to Ireland.

Sometimes overtly, sometimes by more refined and subtle means, pressure is brought to bear on those whose work at times entails public statements critical of government policy. In any case, the programme to combat poverty, in its original form and with its original philosophy, was brought to an abrupt end with minimal consultation. It had become quite clear that the idea of empowering people to participate in the solutions to their own problems meets with hostility when vested interests are threatened.

At one level I suspected that the government wouldn't continue to fund the anti-poverty programme once the EU funding ceased, but I didn't expect the closing would take place the way it did – with no discussion, debate or consultation. It was very disturbing and frustrating because a number of the projects we started around the country had to end – and some very good ideas were lost. Some continued because they found funding elsewhere, but many of the staff we employed lost their jobs when the funding ceased. This was a time of high unemployment in the country, so it was very difficult for those people.

It was not until 1986 (by which time Haughey was temporarily out of power), well over a decade after the establishment of the National Committee on Pilot Schemes to Combat Poverty, that the Combat Poverty Agency itself was established, to advise the government on economic and social policies pertaining to poverty. I was appointed to its board. A key focus of the agency was on supporting community development, and it placed a particular emphasis on tackling child poverty. Its commissioning of research on the definition and extent of poverty was of fundamental importance in establishing benchmarks in our society for income maintenance support.

Combat Poverty did tremendous work over its quarter-century in existence, but it was never popular with the majority party in Irish politics (Fianna Fáil), and it was finally abolished by a government led by Charles Haughey's successor, Bertie Ahern, at the height of the economic boom in Ireland, very shortly before severe recession set in. With our recent slide into deep recession, we are badly in need of an agency to create employment, galvanize communities and work to combat the new poverty that has the nation in its grip, but due to the short-sightedness of Ahern and his party, we no longer have a government agency with that remit. It will be interesting to see if the new coalition government will re-establish the Combat Poverty agency as an independent watchdog to monitor the nature, extent and effect of poverty in these difficult economic times, as inequalities and poverty increase. I believe it should.

Unlike in the 1970s, when the Combat Poverty movement was first instigated, Irish citizens now have extensive access to social rights, services and benefits, but the welfare state in Ireland is incomplete and has not developed in the way it has done in other northern European countries. Even at the height of the economic boom, social and care services were not at the level one would expect in a prosperous society, and services for troubled children, for example, or people with mental illnesses or addictions, were and remain poorly developed. There is limited commitment to universalism in Irish economic thinking, and policies are not aimed at redistribution of resources.

The most marginalized people in our society live in 'consistent poverty'. The Irish government recognizes that a person is living in 'consistent poverty' if they haven't sufficient resources to be able to keep their home adequately warm or cannot afford two good pairs of shoes a year, or to buy Christmas or birthday presents for their family. Even during the economic boom, between 7 and 8 per cent of our people lived in consistent poverty, and up to 10 per cent of our nation's children were in this category. The adults who were and are in consistent poverty are mostly older people, people with long-term illnesses (physical or mental), lone parents, or people caring for a disabled child or other relative. Homeless people fall into this category, as do the long-term unemployed, but so also do some people who work in poorly paid and insecure jobs.

Aside from these very poorest people, we have people whose poverty is not quite so profound, but who are clearly very poor.

They are living a little above the 'consistent poverty' limit, but on less than 60 per cent of the median income in the country. These people wouldn't have much left over to save for a holiday or for Christmas, after paying for their food and accommodation, their heating and utilities, their bus fares and their clothes and occasional treats. And an emergency – such as a family member going into hospital or a washing machine needing replacement – could very easily spiral into financial disaster.

And yet, there is no official recognition of relative income poverty. Officially, people on low levels of income are recognized as being 'at risk' of poverty, but very real financial stress among those who are not categorized as in 'consistent poverty' is not even acknowledged as a form of poverty in its own right. It is as if the government is saying to people living at obviously inadequate income levels that they are in some sort of virtual poverty; that they are not really poor. But it is very real poverty to have to try to manage on inadequate amounts of money. Not only is poverty real for the individuals trying to cope with it, but the numbers living in so-called 'relative' poverty are growing.

It is bad enough to be poor, but to be poor in our consumer society is to be excluded from what is valued by society – from education beyond the basic level and from jobs other than the most badly paid. In our society, those who don't succeed financially, socially and politically are seen as failures, losers, non-productive, useless. It is not good to live your life feeling you are despised by the majority and considered a burden on the state. It does not nurture the self-esteem a person needs in order to function well as a member of a family, a community, a workforce and a society.

Even in the financial mess in which Ireland finds itself at the moment, we are still essentially a rich society; and poor people in a rich society learn to internalize the view of themselves as useless, unproductive and burdensome; this compounds their sense of powerlessness and makes it even more difficult for them to move out of poverty. It is not poor people's actual unworthiness that keeps them poor; but their sense of unworthiness, inculcated through years of being ground down and despised, plays a big role in keeping them down.

One problem is that we have no system that routinely measures poverty in terms of access to healthcare, to housing, to education, to social support and to transport. But even without the statistical information we should have, it is obvious that it is the poorest people who are most affected by difficulties of access to services like these, and the situation of people who are poor is made immeasurably worse by the fact that the public services and social supports they need are inadequate and inaccessible, and in many cases not available at all.

Poor people suffer because the gap between those who can pay for services and those who cannot pay has widened. Those who can pay get what they need; those who can't, don't. This is nowhere more true than in the health service. In spite of its recent affluence, Ireland never recovered from the health cuts of the 1980s, and its provision of healthcare compares poorly with that of other developed countries. Sick people who live on the margins of our society have to wait for treatment, and the waiting lists are often very long. While some people are queuing up for hours on end, sometimes even days, on trolleys or plastic chairs in the accident and emergency departments of our hospitals, others buy their way in the health service, mainly through taking out health insurance, which makes the gap between the public and the private wider and deeper.

The inequity reaches beyond the waiting lists and the A&E bottlenecks. It permeates the system. We have a two-tier health system, which protects middle-class interests, while inequalities are institutionalized. Private patients have their medical care delivered by consultants; public patients receive 'consultant-led' treatment with their care provided mainly by doctors who are still in training, whose working hours are unacceptably long and who may be inexperienced and inadequately supervised.

In recent times there has been increasing reliance on the private sector to provide additional healthcare services. This practice is being promoted as a quicker means to achieve progress. But this trend reinforces unfairness in an already inequitable system. A national healthcare system must have fairness at its core, and it must be based on the recognition that healthcare is an essential service, not a commercial product. It is forty years since Irish society found it possible to eliminate the distinction in the way public and private patients access GP care; it is high time to move towards achieving the same goal in the delivery of hospital care.

The slide into social exclusion really gets under way in school. During the affluent years in Ireland thousands of young people came into second- and third-level education, and yet there is a minority for whom the education system has in fact simply frustrated their potential. These are the 18 per cent of young people in this country who leave school without attaining any qualification at all. They are almost all children from economically and socially deprived communities, and they face the risk of being unemployed or of finding only a poorly paid job in adulthood. Educational disadvantage is an important reason why children who are poor become poor adults. Put in another way, an extremely high proportion (43 per cent) of young people who leave school early are either unemployed or economically inactive, and they find it hard to make up later in life for that lack of education in childhood.

These are mostly children who didn't get on well at school, and who certainly didn't enjoy school. Such children have problems at school mainly because they grow up in poor homes, where there is very little space, money or self-esteem, very low expectations and, consequently, not much motivation to do well at school. It is hardly surprising that children from such homes do not feel very connected to school. They may not have the proper uniform. They may not have a warm coat, or the money for books or the extra things that other children have. Such children start at a disadvantage, especially if they haven't learned, before starting school, through play and encouragement, the key skills of sharing and resolving conflicts peacefully. If they come from very poor homes, they probably have not learned the curiosity that forms the basis of being ready to learn. And so instead of being a place of wonder and fun, school quickly becomes a place of discouragement, and of broken hopes and dreams.

Many children from the poorer homes have difficulty with the discipline required to sit still and to concentrate for long periods. Many never learn to read, or at least not sufficiently well to be able to follow what is going on. The humiliation of feeling that you are seen as weak or stupid or less confident than all the others, who can read, is difficult to handle. And these children who are alienated from school get bored. They cause trouble and get into fights, and gradually the teachers get fed up and see their behaviour, which is really a natural reaction to feeling excluded, as a lack of interest or sheer unruliness.

And so the alienated child begins to miss classes, miss half-days, miss days, and then he comes to be perceived as somebody who cannot benefit from what the school has to offer. The problem is located in the child rather than in the school or the education system, and the child finds himself in a cycle of poor self-esteem that affects everything he thinks about himself and everything he does, maybe for the rest of his life.

These children are quite simply too poor to function at school, too poor to learn to read, too poor to integrate into the life of the school and do well and go on to second or third level. There is so much going on in their lives – so many problems and difficulties – that it is just too hard, too alienating, too depressing to cope with the demands of school as well. And so, for all the excellence of our education system in so many ways, almost 23 per cent of the Irish population are identified as functionally illiterate. This figure represents a failure of the education system, but it also represents what it means to be poor in Ireland today.

The waiting list for social housing is now significantly longer than it was in 1996. Today there are 130,000 households waiting for housing. And while they are on this waiting list, families and individuals depend on the private sector to rent them flats or houses, some living for a long time in bed and breakfasts. That sector is very insecure and tenants are vulnerable. The flats rented to people on the housing list are at the bottom end of the market, where accommodation often lacks essential facilities; some places are not even suitable for human habitation. Here individuals and families who are trapped in poverty have to live in terrible conditions. They may not be actually on the streets and they may not be physically roofless but they are homeless nevertheless, because they lack the very basic constituents of a home. You don't have to be a social activist or a member of a religious order – indeed, you don't need to be wedded to any belief or theory at all – to know that this is simply unacceptable.

In addition to those nominally housed but effectively homeless, there are 5,000 people in Ireland who are actually and literally homeless, over 800 of whom are children. They live in temporary or emergency accommodation. In other words, they are wandering around and living by going from hostel to hostel or even sleeping on the streets. What makes all of these figures even more shocking is that these dramatic increases in housing needs have taken place at a time when we have been building more houses than ever before. Currently, there are almost 300,000 vacant houses across the country – nearly 15 per cent of the housing stock. Yet despite the over-production of houses and the number of homes lying empty, thousands of people are living day to day in inadequate housing conditions. They continue to be denied one of their most basic human rights: the right to a place they can call home.

We have made some efforts to combat homelessness in Ireland. Additional hostel places have been made available recently and some have been modernized. But despite these improvements, there are homeless people who still have to sleep rough at night because all the emergency accommodation is full.

Some hostels provide inappropriate accommodation in dormitories, where drug-free young people have to sleep next to drug users and where vulnerable homeless people have to share facilities with career criminals. In such places, the homeless sleep with their shoes under their pillow for fear they will be stolen during the night. There are still emergency services for homeless people that infringe their dignity and fuel their frustration and anger.

Private rented accommodation has traditionally been a route out of homelessness. However, as the cost of housing escalated in recent years, so also did the cost of rented accommodation. Rents have come down recently, in line with falling property values, but decent accommodation is still out of the reach of many. Homeless people are entitled to a rent supplement from the state towards the cost of renting private accommodation, but there is a limit to the amount the state is willing to contribute, and there are plans as I write to reduce this already inadequate amount.

To make matters worse, the state will not always agree to pay the deposit (equivalent to four weeks' rent) that is required in advance, and in any case it can be extremely difficult to find landlords who are willing to accept tenants reliant on welfare payments. For all these reasons, the escape route of private rented accommodation is very limited. Some homeless people who have the patience to persevere for weeks and months may manage, with the support of one of the voluntary agencies, to acquire settled accommodation, but it is increasingly difficult.

A better route out of homelessness is social housing, but the waiting lists for local authority accommodation are growing, and the wait can be anything up to five years, which means that homeless people find it more and more difficult to get access to social housing. Single homeless people are constantly being pushed to the very bottom of the waiting list, since priority is given to families with children, and single men may simply never get local authority accommodation.

According to the government's 2008 Homelessness Strategy, *The Way Home*, and commitments made in its programme for government, 2010 was to be the year that long-term homelessness was due to come to an end. Of course, this was before the economic crash, and now as I write, it is clear that the government's own target for ending homelessness has not been met.

There is an alternative. People do not have to be homeless. People do not have to be in housing need. People do not have to live in relative or consistent poverty. These human realities are the results of choices made by government, by business and by society as a whole. We need a new social and economic model that promotes economic equality and targets those who have benefited the least during the boom, and who are now suffering the most in the recession.

Immigrants have made a huge contribution to Irish society in recent years, through taking up jobs where there were labour shortages; once they became established in our system, they contributed, and continue to contribute, like everyone else by paying their taxes. They also have an important contribution to make to the social and cultural life of the country. Despite our long history of emigration, we in Ireland are relatively new players on the immigration scene and we are slow to recognize that when we look for workers it is human beings who come. We have to learn that the human person who comes to this country to fill a job vacancy is not just an economic unit, but a person who has needs – and not only economic but social, political, spiritual and psychological needs. Migrant workers were very welcome in Ireland when we had labour shortages, but there was little protection of their rights as workers. Since the economy started to fail, many migrant workers have left Ireland, but those who have remained and settled here continue to experience many problems: for example families separated by migration have no statutory right to family reunification. Many other migrants who have lived here for many years have difficulty in getting long-term residency status or citizenship. This makes migrant workers feel very insecure.

For asylum seekers it is worse again. While their cases are being processed – which can go on sometimes for many years – asylum seekers have to live under the 'direct provision' system, which means that they are supplied with accommodation, food and basic necessities and a very small amount of spending money, but they are not allowed to work. For people who have provided for themselves and their families all their lives, this is demeaning and frustrating. Ireland is one of only a few EU countries that refuse to allow asylum seekers to take up employment – which makes no sense to me. How can these people make a genuine contribution to our society if they are prevented from working, from paying taxes, from paying their way – the very thing for which they are criticized?

It's important for a country like Ireland to remember that immigrants are not free-standing individuals. They are members of families and belong to various social networks. They are rooted in a culture and a tradition. They have ties to home and homeland. We need a coherent and cohesive long-term strategy for immigrants. We need a rights-based approach to immigration: we need to recognize immigrants' right to family reunification and their right to long-term residency. We need also to recognize their right to integrate into our society. We need to allow people to cherish their own culture while also learning to respect Irish culture; in other words, we need to develop integration policies that are based on shared values.

For decades we were told that we had to create wealth before we could distribute it. When we had wealth in this country, however, we had no proposals to redistribute it. There are no plans to engage in any comprehensive redistribution that would improve the social protection we provide and that would take everybody out of consistent poverty and reduce to close to zero those in relative poverty. Unless there is a radical change in our policies and priorities, the situation of people living in poverty will continue, with the poor becoming more marginalized. The reason for this is that poverty is not just a by-product of poor economic performance. Poverty is built into the way our society operates. I am not just talking about consistent and relative poverty. I am also talking about housing poverty, health poverty and education poverty. As long as society operates on the principle of individualism and personal achievement, poverty will not be eradicated. What we need is a strong social policy and an agenda which will ensure that we have equitable distribution of our resources.

I believe there remains very deep in the Irish psyche a profound commitment to Christian values, to community, generosity, fairness and justice – and a profound suspicion of values that are entirely individualistic. The Church can play a crucial role in highlighting, living and promoting these values.

The challenge for our policy-makers is to ensure that the benefits of what wealth we can generate are distributed across health, housing, welfare, education and transport in a way that will ensure all our citizens are served with equal respect and according to their needs. This is not how we operate at the moment. We have become a class-conscious society. We are wealth-conscious, and we are afraid of losing any of our comforts. But standards of living in developed countries cannot be equated with levels of disposable income. If we are to enjoy a good standard of living, everyone must be able to access good-quality services as the need arises. The problem with focusing on making sure that people have a higher disposable income is that this simply supports inequality: the more income people have to spend, the more likely they are to buy their way out of poor-quality public services. Paying for services in the private sector solves the immediate problem for those concerned, but it also creates inequality, because for people who live on the margins of society it is not an option, and never will be an option.

If we want to bring people from the margins into the centre, we must come up with new ideas about how we organize society economically, socially and politically. To nurture such new ideas we need to encourage debate, and encouraging debate means that we must overcome the profound anti-intellectualism of our political structures and culture.

During the boom years we had an opportunity to eliminate long-term poverty and restructure services and the economic system so that people would have equal access to the services they need, but we did not take that opportunity when we had it. Now that we are in deep recession in Ireland, the taxpayer has been forced to bail out the failed banking system, and severe cuts have been made in public service pay and in services at all levels in society. While the previous government promised to eliminate poverty by 2012, the present government is noticeably silent with regard to poverty or its elimination.

While the economy was booming, we somehow managed to convince ourselves that everyone was better off. The rising economic tide would raise all boats and lift everyone out of poverty, the argument went. There is of course some validity to this, and it is true that with increased prosperity, we did reduce our levels of absolute poverty. However, experience has taught us that we cannot rely on the rising economic tide to lift every boat – some boats are simply much more buoyant than others – and the boats that get left behind, lodged in poverty and exclusion, present problems for the rest of the flotilla that will not go away if we just wait long enough for the tide to rise again. And now, even the greatest and most affluent ocean liners have foundered. The idea that the marketplace and economic growth can be relied upon to take care of redistributing wealth has been well and truly discredited.

We must take a clear look at our society and consider our situation afresh, as happened forty years ago with the Kilkenny Conference on Poverty, which had such an influence on public and political thinking for many years. We need a public debate on the type of society we want and the values which should underpin that society. If such a discussion were to take place, civil society could make a valuable contribution from the perspective of the marginalized. I believe perhaps a large number of community and locally based projects working with people in poverty and the people themselves could do so too.

This is our responsibility as citizens. It is not just the government's responsibility. It is up to all of us to press for these changes. It is vitally important that we take ownership of our responsibility as citizens. The gap between individualism and community-mindedness will only be filled if we have a sense of ownership. It is our time, our place, right here now in this village, in this neighbourhood, in this town, in this city. Imagine what it would be like, and how exciting it would be, if every village, every parish, every town was discussing and debating the type of society we want, and the values of fairness, justice and compassion which would underpin that society. What happens here and now is our responsibility; what happens tomorrow is our legacy. We are all responsible for the time we live in. We hold that responsibility jointly and we hold it now.

5

Focus on Homelessness

Bishop Birch's sudden and untimely death in 1981 came like a bolt from the blue. My soul was filled with a grief and a sorrow that I had never known before. His death seemed unbearable for a time. As well as a dear friend, I had lost the person who was the source of my inspiration. I was, quite simply, devastated, and I knew I needed time to grieve.

During this time I was fortunate to have the support of the community, colleagues and friends. They seemed to understand the depth of my sorrow and gave me the space and the time to mourn my loss. It took a good six or seven months before I felt I could gather myself together again – and looking back I know that without the support I received I would not have been able to survive and move on.

But sad though my loss was at the time, in a sense it was a beginning as well as an ending; it was the beginning of a new phase of my life and I knew I had to discover for myself where God was drawing me.

With Jean Vanier, the charismatic founder of L'Arche, an international
movement concerned with the welfare of people.

Later that year, Jean Vanier, founder of L'Arche (an international movement concerned with the care of people with
intellectual disabilities), whom I had met through Peter Birch
some years earlier, came to visit, and with his visit the clouds
began to lift. I had always been influenced by Jean's work and his
commitment, but now he became my soul-guide and my inspiration. Living the Gospel in the L'Arche fraternity, committed
totally to the restoration of a broken universe and acknowledging
the special place of handicapped people in that restoration,
he sustained, encouraged and guided me in the way of God's
love, as my spiritual director and through the annual eight-day
retreats that he led, to find my strength in my weaknesses in

the bright and dark days and years of the 1980s and 1990s.

Sisters were often moved, which is what we do and expect as part of a religious life. But when I left Kilkenny it was a difficult time for me – and how this move came about didn't help at all. At that stage it was normal in our congregation that when sisters were moved from one place to another, there was a process of consultation and discernment by the provincial leader and the sister concerned. This didn't happen in my case.

In October 1982 I did as was usual at that time of the year and developed a draft plan for the social services for the coming year; this had to be approved by the management committee and the bishop who had replaced Peter Birch. When I went to see the bishop with the draft plan he seemed surprised, and informed me that he understood that I would not be in Kilkenny the follow-ing year. He was equally surprised that I hadn't heard this news from the provincial leader. Somewhat shocked, I contacted the provincial leader to find out exactly what was happening and she acknowledged that she had met the bishop and had told him of the move. I was hurt that my leaving Kilkenny had been discussed with the bishop before it was discussed with me, and I told her so. When it was announced publicly that I was leaving there was great media interest and a lot of suggestions in the national media that I was being moved because the new bishop didn't want me, and to this day I don't know what conversation took place between the bishop and the provincial, but I was told I was leav-ing Kilkenny, and that is what I did.

I left Kilkenny, a place that I had grown to love, for Dublin in the spring of 1983, and although it was with sorrow, it was also

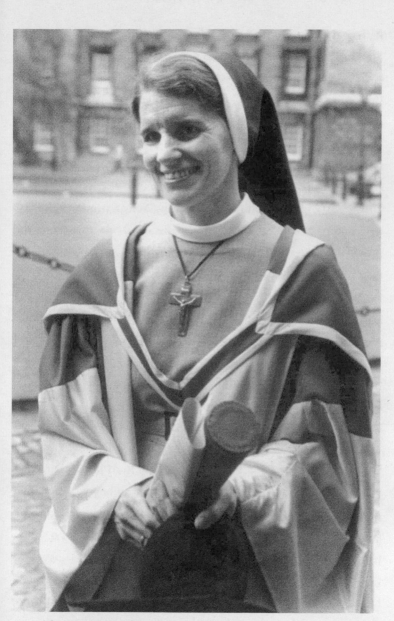

After receiving my honorary doctorate from Trinity College, 1982.

with a trust in God who, I felt, was leading me forward and drawing me on. I attended the general chapter of the Sisters of Charity that summer, and that opened new windows of hope. Reflecting on the spirit of Mary Aikenhead, we challenged each other again to listen to the cry of the poor and break the walls of prejudice and fear that protect our security and limit our vision.

By October of that year I was a senior research fellow at University College Dublin, undertaking research into homelessness amongst women. I'd had permission to do this from the provincial leader and moving into this area offered me not only a new opportunity to study, but the chance to reflect on my own experience in the active ministry. I was quite familiar with the Social Science Department of UCD and the staff there, who were a very great support to me, so in a sense I was moving into another community. But it was very different from living and working with the people in Kilkenny whom I loved and who had become such an important part of my life.

As far as the public was concerned, there were very few homeless women in Dublin at this time, and those who did exist were believed to be mainly eccentric 'bag ladies'. But I knew that there was a much bigger homelessness problem among women than people thought. I knew, for example, that young girls coming from rural Ireland to Dublin often had nowhere to live and sometimes ended up becoming involved in prostitution. I also knew that there were long-term homeless women, abandoned by their families, living out their lives in institutions. I felt drawn to find out more about women's homelessness, and to do something about it.

Kilkenny Social Services and the time I spent there continued to be the inspiration for my work in Dublin. I knew from the Kilkenny experience that people when they set about it purposefully could be influential in bringing about change. My aspiration for my new project was radically different from the traditional response to poor people in the sense that I was determined to provide the best services I possibly could, 'to provide for the poor what the rich can buy with money', as Mother Mary Aikenhead had put it more than a century previously.

My first move was to become a 'student'. I carried out a study on the nature and extent of homelessness amongst women in Dublin and had eight research assistants – funded through a FAS scheme (Foras Áiseanna Saothair, the state funded national training programme) – to help me. The study examined the characteristics of these women, the way they had become homeless in the first place, and the provisions made for them. I also conducted interviews with the women, carried out focus group discussions and used participant observations, where I and some of the researchers spent time with them in hostels, bus shelters, or on the streets – wherever they were – in order to gauge their circumstances and their needs.

We discovered that the typical homeless woman did not exist. She may be dossing, squatting or depending on the goodwill of friends and family. She may be young and a runaway who's been thrown out of her home and is struggling to support herself; she may be a victim of domestic violence, hiding away from an abusive husband in a hostel and battling to provide for her children; she may be an older woman living in an institution because she has nowhere else to go. What united all these women was not so much their homelessness as the appalling lack of emergency accommodation, their limited rights to public housing and the lack of statutory rights to a decent home. This was the first study to be carried out on homeless women in Ireland and what it highlighted was a dark and deeply depressing rejection of women in society.

Central to our study was a new approach: instead of offering them what we thought they ought to have, we chose instead to listen to them, as they told their stories. This attitude of respectful listening was informed by the action-research approach to social issues. My experience on the Committee to Combat Poverty had made me aware of new approaches to social services and community development, including in particular action-research. This method perceives research and action as interlinked: action is driven by research, and research in turn influences action. Action-research is characterized by the engagement of the researcher with the action. The research identifies the people that are in need of services, the type of services they need and the strategies that are likely to be of use, and the findings of the research are then used as the basis for action. This action, along with analysis of the political context and critical reflection, is used to develop policies and strategies to respond to needs and present evidence to government and relevant agencies. This approach contrasts radically with traditional measures to combat poverty in Ireland, whereby the problems of the poor were alleviated either through charity or through a state intervention model where experts or professionals intervened without the active participation of the poor.

In line with this kind of thinking, I believed that the personal stories of homeless women would provide the basis for the design of services to meet their needs. I wanted to know who was in the homeless population, what caused women to become homeless and, once homeless, what would help women to move out of homelessness. Armed with this information, I felt I would then be in a position to develop a strategy and mobilize support. And that was the basis for my research project.

The eight research assistants I had in that first year were all wonderfully enthusiastic, intelligent and generous young women. Among them was Rachel Collier, with whom I was to work for many years to come in Focus Point and Focus Ireland. Rachel was a gifted young woman and was totally committed to the work. She was very generous and contributed greatly in the development of the organization. Working long hours on what was then a very low wage, and never counting the cost, Rachel took the risk of forfeiting a promising career in journalism and voluntarily embarked on this mission without knowing where it would lead us.

At first, the research project operated from a room in Stanhope Street in the north of Dublin, in a building that had been part of the very convent where I lived as a young nun, when I first came to Dublin. We later moved to rented premises right in the city centre, which we shared with the Prisoners Rights Organisation. There we compiled the research findings, wrote up the study and prepared it for publication. Later again we moved to premises in Eustace Street, in what is now the trendy Temple Bar area of Dublin, but at that time was a run-down and semi-derelict place. The Sisters of Charity paid the rent for the first year and gave me a loan of £5,000 to get me started – but all other funding, I had to find. Later that year, I set up a fund-raising committee, and negotiated with various government departments to get funding. In that first year I managed to get one department to pay the salaries of two outreach workers who worked the streets at night making contact with young homeless people. Today, a quarter of a century on, Focus Ireland's flagship coffee shop and advice centre is still based in Eustace Street.

The findings of our research confirmed my conviction that there were far more homeless women than anyone had realized. In discovering 'hidden homelessness', we challenged the popular belief that there were few if any homeless women in Dublin. Indeed, we found that there were over 500 women we called the visible homeless, and when 'hidden homelessness' was taken into

The bustling Focus Ireland coffee shop opens on Eustace Street, 1987.

consideration, the estimate of the total number of homeless women in Dublin ran into thousands. This was a staggering finding.

The most visible part of the female homeless population were those who used hostels that offered emergency accommodation to women. As part of the research, researchers were placed in these emergency hostels. They were appalled at what they saw. We found that the hostels were not fully occupied, even though so many women were in need of accommodation. From discussions with homeless women, and our own observation, we began to understand why many women would not use hostels. Although they provided basic food and shelter, conditions in the hostels were way below standard. They were cold and regimented, and the women using them were not supported to move out of homelessness and into secure, affordable accommodation. Perhaps they felt that once in they would be stuck and unable to get out – that they had no prospect of ever leaving these harsh surroundings.

Younger women in particular didn't want to go into those hostels. They didn't want to be controlled or get stuck in them. They knew instinctively what home meant – a place of warmth and security, safety and stability – and seemed anxious to make sure I understood that they *did* have homes of their own – and that this is where they belonged. They would never use the word 'homeless' in relation to themselves, and that's why we introduced a new term: 'being out of home' – which meant having a home but not being able to go there.

The 'invisible' homeless women included those who didn't want to use the hostels and who instead coped with their homelessness by moving from one form of accommodation to another, in the private rented sector, doubling up with friends, and maybe ending up in squats. One reason for the relative invisibility of homeless women is that, being more vulnerable than men, women tend to keep quiet and in the shadows, in case drawing attention to themselves might lead to trouble.

In identifying these women as homeless, we were drawing attention not just to a whole unidentified group of homeless people, but to the nature of home itself – it is not merely a place of shelter, as the institutions housing these forgotten women undoubtedly were, but a place where a person feels safe and secure and where they can have some influence on their own domestic arrangements; a place, in short, where a person *feels* at home. This understanding of home was to become a foundation stone of the Focus Ireland project.

The research project, as well as revealing the extent of female homelessness, identified the causes of homelessness as a combination of personal and structural problems. The structural causes identified were mainly poverty and lack of housing. Decent housing was hard to come by. The public housing that was on offer to homeless people was substandard, and the supply of flats and houses for rent at reasonable rates from private landlords had begun to dry up. Another structural problem was the lack of suitable follow-on arrangements for people leaving institutional care.

Personal problems compound structural ones, and the research found that a crisis – such as a family dispute, an illness, loss of a job, a death, an eviction, a fire, a pregnancy or family violence – could push a woman on to the streets. When some of these factors were put together with not having enough money to pay rent, and not having the information, advice and support services that might help a person to find a suitable place to live, it became very difficult for people to break out of the cycle of homelessness.

Another insight gained from this study was that the reasons people become homeless are often different from the reasons they remain homeless, and this insight remains to this day a major part of Focus Ireland's thinking about homelessness. Once on the streets, women found that their choices were limited if they did not have the economic resources to move out of homelessness. For women, life on the streets could mean exploitation and involvement in petty crime and prostitution. In the absence of alternatives, many women were returning to violent partners where they endured further degradation and exploitation.

Although the study found that women were often very resilient and determined to try to improve their situation, it also found that drifting in and out of homelessness led to low self-esteem and meant pain, marginalization and powerlessness.

Inspired by the women themselves, and with a donation from the Religious Sisters of Charity to pay the rent for one year and a loan of £5,000, I decided to continue working with a core group of homeless women after the initial research project had come to an end. I wanted to listen to them, to hear their stories, and to try to understand homelessness from the point of view of homeless people themselves, so that we could better respond to their needs.

The core group comprised eight homeless women: two Marys, Bernie, Kathleen, Julie, Michelle, Colette and Carrie. Most of these women had lost contact with their families, their relatives and their friends. They were bravely surviving alone in a world that offered them little but demanded a great deal of suffering. As well as the eight women, I had a small team of research assistants: Noleen Fox, Rosemary Cullen, and Rachel Collier who had been involved in the earlier research project. They were later joined by Síle Wall and Trish Murphy. They were all greatly enthusiastic about the research and put all their skills, talents and energies into making it work. Without their help and support things would have been very difficult for me.

This small group of people with different experiences tried to explore the meaning of homelessness, what had to be done about it and what supports people out of home needed to secure a home of their own. I was convinced – and my conversations with the women strengthened this conviction – that any new approach to the provision of housing for homeless people should take as a basic principle that homeless people should not be expected to live in conditions that providers were not prepared to live in themselves. Indeed, the poor conditions and meagre supports available to homeless women were part of the problem that kept women homeless.

We spent the following year listening to and being led and taught by the eight young women who had been homeless. I did not know where I was being led, but I knew deep in my heart that the wisdom of the Spirit was speaking to me through these women, the rejected ones, who inspired me to dream of a world without homelessness. It was a year of exploring, examining, understanding and discovering the deeper meaning of being out of home. Eating, listening, reading, writing, crying and laughing, we shared our songs, poems, plays, joys and sorrows, hopes and fears, pains and struggles, the secrets of our souls. I came to realize that everyone who has been deeply hurt has the right to be sure that they are loved, that we all need a comforting presence to bring peace, hope and life, and that we all need and have a right to a place called home.

During that year I also learned in a very special way the wisdom of the excluded, the rejected, the women out of home, and I learned to let that wisdom guide me in a way I knew not. Their wisdom continued to guide me in the years ahead. They knew the pain of powerlessness, homelessness, poverty and rejection. They knew what it was to be treated without dignity, respect or grace and they knew deep want and the suffering caused by injustice, greed and power. They knew it in their minds and hearts, in their bodies and in their bones, in the deepest part of their being. But they also knew how things could be different.

The women described in great detail their life of homelessness and what it was like for them not to be able to go home. How awful it was not to have an address, a place where they could leave their things, a place to wash, to change their clothes. How awful it was not to be able to shut the door behind them and to have privacy.

What was even worse was the lack of respect. They described vividly how people's faces would change when they heard the word homeless. They described how dejected and rejected they felt, and how their whole sense of themselves was eroded day by day.

They did get help when they looked for it – clothes, food,

money – but always they felt that what they got was second hand, second rate, leftovers. What was not good enough for other people. So even as they were being helped they felt disrespected. Their cry for respect, this need to be treated decently and for good and equitable relationships with other people, touched me and opened my heart. I began to discover how poor people feel they are a burden on society, and a disappointment to their families. How sensitive their hearts are, and how capable they are of warmth and tenderness. They are waiting for someone who is willing and open enough to love them, and someone who will meet them where they are.

One of the most important things I learned from my work with poor and vulnerable people is that they know better than anybody else what they need. They are absolutely clear about this. They can teach us what they need. It was through listening to them that I came to realize that anyone providing services to these people must ensure that what is provided is of good quality and a high standard. It is only poor people themselves who know, from experience, how offensive it is to be given a poor service just because they are poor. From listening to poor people I realized that for those of us who work to provide services to poor people, what we are called upon to provide is a quality service, delivered with respect, so that people using it can receive it with dignity. These insights became the cornerstone of the new organization, which we named Focus Point, later Focus Ireland.

During that year a new movement was being conceived, almost without our knowing it. As we set about deciding on a name for the new organization, I knew that I too needed a 'focus', a groundedness. And as we named the values that would underpin Focus Point, I too, with the women, named hospitality, safety, security, structure, empowerment, compassion, equality, respect and dignity. We discovered how alike we all were in our common humanity, our giftedness, the frailty at the root of our creature-hood. That year had a profound effect on my life. I was helped to move into a sense of deep gratitude to and reverence for these women for all they taught me about myself, about humanity and about society, and gratitude to God for drawing me close to them and to him through them.

With six of the original eight homeless women and the women who walked with them – Mary, Kathleen, Michelle, Julie, Bernie, Carrie, Rosemary, Rachel, Síle, Trish, Maura and myself, with a strong fundraising committee and a very committed management board under the chairmanship of Peter Kelly – Focus Point opened its doors and its heart to homeless people in September 1985. By providing the services identified by homeless women during the previous two years, we were bringing dignity on to the street, and were determined to end long-term homelessness, believing that homelessness should be a stage, and not a state.

6

Leading Change

In my view, the first thing you have to do as a leader is to listen. And anybody who wants to be in leadership in the voluntary sector should listen to the people who are on the margins, because they understand society much better than those of us who are in the middle of it.

The vision of Focus Ireland is that everybody has a right to a place called home. This vision grew out of my research in UCD, and then the work I did in the following year listening to those young women who had been homeless in Dublin. The year I spent learning from those eight women was the greatest year of my life, because I really did grow to understand what it was like to be out of home. They taught me that no matter what else we did, we had to develop a service that would restore people's pride, their respect, their self-esteem. And it was from them I learned what it was that homeless people most needed: a 24-hour phone service to contact for information; a place for people to drop into to get information and advice; a place where women could get good food at a reasonable price, where they could relax and feel safe from street values. (It was mostly men who used the dinner centres and there was a lot of aggression and violence, so women were afraid to go there.) They also said it would be good to have people on the streets who would reach out to homeless people. So those were exactly the services we established when we started Focus. We tried to have an organization that would be inclusive, that would include them not just as people using the service but as people whose experience was informing the kinds of services we would provide.

My experience helping Bishop Birch to develop Kilkenny Social Services influenced my work in Dublin. It was from him that I learned the value of listening to the people you want to create services for, and trying to meet the actual needs they identify. It was also from my experience in Kilkenny that I came to understand the importance of including volunteers in this kind of work, and I always try to ensure that volunteers have a proper place in work I am involved in, complementing the professionals. As organizations grow and become more formal, they tend to become less reliant on and less committed to working with volunteers, but in my view, volunteers are not just a stopgap solution while an organization is developing its professional staff. Volunteers bring an altruistic spirit to the work that is very valuable, and can be a positive influence on professional staff as well. Focus Ireland has always included volunteers, and I am very grateful for their contribution.

Another thing I learned early on was that people need a lot of support in their work. If you want an organization to develop, you must ensure that people have the right kind of skills and you need to help them to find the appropriate training and education. Again, I learned that from Bishop Birch. I helped to set up the School of Social Education in Kilkenny, which became a training centre for childcare workers. I brought this experience into my work in Focus and other organizations I worked in. I always tried to ensure that staff got opportunities to be trained and that they had the right kind of supervision and support to enable them to give their best. Having a good system of support and supervision makes a good organization.

In selecting staff, their talents and gifts are important. It is also important that they complement mine. But talents and gifts without drive and ambition are not enough, just as drive and ambition without talents and gifts are not enough.

There are four things that are very important to me as I try to develop an organization: not being afraid of change; having a great curiosity; being interested in the big picture; and being happy with small successes. A combination of these qualities with a driving sense of purpose is for me critically important.

Leaders in the voluntary sector have to have a good understanding of the society in which we live and the systems we have. They also need to see beyond their own organization to the wider picture and have the capacity to think outside the box. In particular, we must be able to let go when we have done certain work – it is better if we can pass it on. For example, if the state is prepared to do it, then we in the voluntary sector should move on to the next thing.

At an organizational level, leadership in the voluntary sector has to be co-operative. From the earliest days, I tried to ensure that that spirit was at the core of Focus Ireland, because I believed voluntary organizations couldn't afford to be in competition with one another and instead should see the complementarities of each other's work. That makes giving and gaining the co-operation of others very important.

When I was in college, I was told that you should define the problem and then develop the response. But now I think, and this is an insight I got from my experience, that it is actually only when people see that there is a solution – a way out – that they can see the problem. Understanding this about human nature is very valuable for the kind of work I have been engaged in all my life. Developing solutions and showing a way to fix a problem is most definitely the best way to gain support and resources. It is announcing as well as denouncing – and if you announce as you denounce you are more effective.

An example of helping people to see problems by showing them a solution was in our work with young people. During the study on homeless women and even as I was setting up Focus Point, I was not aware that there were children under 18 years of age out on their own without their parents. But very soon after we opened the coffee shop, people as young as 12 and 13 came to our services. There was nothing else for them – nowhere else they could turn to for help. The sense of abandonment they experienced left them open to exploitation by others; they often had problems accepting traditional structured settings while trying to cope with personal traumas. They became enmeshed in street culture, and because of this they often became more difficult to reach and to provide for.

But although they were coming to the coffee shop and the day centre, there wasn't a place for them at night. Putting accommodation in place was a big project and would have cost a quarter of a million a year to run. That was a lot of money in 1990. For three years we tried everything we could think of to get the Department of Health to agree to undertake this, but they couldn't seem to see the problem.

In the end, I asked the Sisters of Charity to give money for one year, and premises, which they did. Once that had been agreed, I used it as leverage with the Department. I told the Minister, Chris Flood, that the money and premises were available on condition that if the work was successful, the government would continue to fund it. He agreed and at the end of the year the Department of Health did fund and support us, and continues to do so to this day. Of course the centre has been full since it opened and many more centres have opened since.

It's not enough to show people the solutions, though. It's also important to identify the right people to approach in order to get what it is that you need. Some people are never going to see the point of some kinds of services, whereas others will row in behind you on certain issues where they can see that your proposed solutions could work. Then again, those same people might not see the value of a different idea, and you need to look elsewhere then for support. So knowing what people are interested in and what they are likely to support is a key skill for anyone who is trying to bring about change.

It's also important to be aware that people like to see success, and they like to see that what they are supporting works. For this reason, it's good to find ways to show people that what they're supporting is valuable. We owe that to those who support us, whether financially or in other ways. We owe it to them to let them know that they brought this about. In the development of an organization, building capacity to grow is very important, as is developing models of hope, and helping people to see that no good deed or good thing ever dies.

7

Home from Home

Focus Point's work grew and extended, and in a short time we complemented our crisis services by providing good-quality housing for vulnerable people who otherwise could not afford it. Stanhope Street Convent, where I was first missioned in the early 1960s, was to become the site of our first housing project, made possible by the donation of the convent building by the Sisters of Charity. This was where Mary Aikenhead had lived during the early years of the congregation, establishing her first novitiate there in 1819.

In need of premises for a housing project I had in mind, I asked the order for the convent. They gave it, because they were planning a move to a smaller building anyway, but I had no money to renovate it, and it was like a millstone around my neck for about six months. I was afraid that if I didn't get the work on the building started, squatters might move in, and then we would not be able to proceed. Although it might sound contradictory for someone trying to alleviate homelessness to want to remove

On her last day in office, President Mary Robinson took the time to formally open the new Focus Ireland housing development in George's Hill, 1997.

squatters, I knew that once I had the go-ahead for the major reconstruction work to be done on the convent, I had to move fast.

The plan was to provide one-bedroom apartments where tenants would have their own living room and bedroom, their own kitchen and bathroom, and their own front door. We would provide accommodation and the support staff on the campus to enable the tenants to live as independently as possible. Many of the tenants had mental health needs and couldn't manage to live totally independently, so it was important to offer them the support they needed.

As I mentioned previously, the transitional housing was meant for young families who needed help with the running of the house and the rearing of their children. The idea for this came about through my previous experience as a student working in Cupar in Fife (Scotland). This was a pilot scheme involving a small number of houses where whole families were taken into care; the children were not separated from their parents and the scheme appeared to work very well.

So I went to the Department of the Environment, which dealt with housing. Supportive housing for homeless people was a new idea. Homeless people were generally cared for in temporary hostels and shelters and people found it difficult to grasp the idea of supportive housing. I returned again and again to the Minister Padraig Flynn for funding for the conversion of Stanhope Street Convent into supportive housing for homeless people. Finally the Minister announced and provided a million pounds for the project. I will never know if this commitment to fund the new housing project was based on conviction, pity or political expedience, but having been given the money we were able to provide the first social housing project for homeless people in Ireland. We converted the old convent building into eighty one-bedroomed apartments and ten houses – known as Stanhope Green – for transitional housing for families.

Transitional housing was another very new idea at the time. Meeting families who came to our drop-in centre, we found there were many who couldn't manage to create and maintain a home without support. We started by helping them in their homes, but this was not enough, so then we came up with the idea of providing transitional housing, whereby they would spend six months in a house in Stanhope Green and get all sorts of support, training and education to help them to manage their home and their children; this project proved to be a wonderful success and became a model for many other projects.

Later the Presentation and Holy Faith Sisters also made property available to us for people who would otherwise be unhoused. The Focus work continued to expand and develop over the years, and by 1994 we were starting to move outside Dublin to help local communities in provincial towns and cities that were working to provide supportive housing and other supportive services for people with housing needs.

The Focus story is a story about people, wonderful people, giving and receiving. It is the story of bringing into the light the hidden lives of many. It is a story of adventure, risk, dynamic activity and self-giving. It is a story about development and growth. Focus Ireland is now a large organization with dozens of projects in Dublin and around Ireland, and is recognized as a centre of expertise and good practice in the provision of services and housing to homeless people. It ministers to thousands of homeless men, women, young people and children in crisis every year. Services, activities, houses, communities, self-help, giving, receiving, research, publications, protests, marches, campaigns, celebrations, reflection, miracles, joy and laughter are all part of life at Focus Ireland. It brings hope, life, love, safety, respect, structure, security, rights and dignity into all our lives.

But it is also a story of suffering, sickness, struggle, injustice, oppression, being let down, being put down. When things were going well, I rejoiced, and when things weren't going so well, I often felt deflated, and then I sat and wept. Then came change – an inspiration, a prayer, a rest, a word, a friend, reflection, a sabbatical, a retreat – and winter changed to spring, forces awakened, life seemed to surge once more, bringing the unswerving certainty that I should go on with determination and joy. I knew that I carried within me all the weakness and frailties of humankind as well as all the possibilities for growth and development.

Through all this, I learned about my own vulnerability and human frailties. I have learned that human frailties, which I fear, and which I try to run from, to wipe out, to cover up, are my saving grace. These human frailties that have humbled and at times even humiliated me have also held me up and reminded me again and again that I have absolutely no right to point the finger at any human being. It is precisely these frailties that led me and drew me to walk with God and with the poor.

Each day I become more aware that I am not complete, not

finished, not self-sustaining. This knowledge can make one fearful and guarded, but I know it can force me to make room and space in my heart for God's love and grace and the gift of my brothers and sisters, especially those who are most excluded. I have learned that my strongest solidarity with the poor comes about only to the degree to which I am willing to enter into the mystery of my own frail, fragile and at times uncontrollable humanity. It is the neediness and poverty of my humanity that ties me to all humanity and that brings me the gifts of faith, hope and love. It is when I am most secure, most strong, most powerful, most in control, that I am most weak and empty and it is when I am weak that I am strong.

There came a point, in the 1990s, when Focus Ireland was alive, strong and healthy, and I knew it. I had spent ten years leading the organization, and I felt it was important that Focus Ireland would – and I knew that it could – continue well without me at the helm, and without depending on me into the future. And so I made way for others to take over, realizing that it was time for me to be with the organization in a new way. That small voice within reminded me that I was now in my fifties, and the time had come to search anew for a different way to be present to the poor. I still carried within me the seeds of contemplation, waiting to be nurtured, wounds waiting to be healed, rocks waiting to be moved, a body awaiting rest, ideas waiting to be realized, gifts waiting to be claimed and reclaimed, the mystic and artist waiting to be matured, God's work of art awaiting a different kind of stroke. I stood again with myself and my God, to learn afresh where I was being drawn, with the same faith and trust with which I left the

Dingle peninsula for Dublin, Dublin for Kilkenny, and Kilkenny for Dublin again, believing, like the American poet Adrienne Rich, that, 'Our gifts compel/ Master our ways and lead us in the end/ Where we are most ourselves'.

In 1993 I made two decisions: one was to take a sabbatical for nine months. The second decision was to resign as the head of Focus – a difficult decision, but one based on my experiences in Kilkenny. There I had realized that no organization should depend on one person – and the only way to ensure that it grew and developed was to enable other people to take charge of it and move it forward.

After I made provision with the board for my replacement during my absence, I headed to California on sabbatical. But even this wasn't without its problems, for whilst it was exciting to be free of work, I soon discovered that moving from huge responsibility to having none at all was not plain sailing. In fact, I found it very challenging. I'd lived with a packed schedule for so long that doing nothing at all – or even trying to establish another, less stressful routine – was too much for me, and I felt completely lost and alone. My sleep pattern changed, and I found it difficult to relax into this new way of living.

It took about three months – and the help of a good friend of mine from college – to make the necessary adjustment and start to enjoy my time off. Once I got the hang of this new life, I relished the freedom – the freedom to simply be – to think, without responsibilities and duties – and it gave me the opportunity to be creative, to spend time reading, to write, to go to the theatre or listen to music. I was able to visit wonderful places, such as Yosemite National Park and the Grand Canyon. I even went skiing!

I also participated in debates, discussions and lectures on spirituality and theology. It was as if this time away opened my eyes, and my heart, to a new world – and I felt renewed, spiritually, psychologically and physically.

My sabbatical was a great help to me when I returned to Ireland. Although no longer in charge of Focus, I became involved with developing the organization at a national level.

There were challenging years during the 1990s for Focus Ireland, as it looked to the future and worked to strengthen its structures and systems and build up its management. But Focus Ireland rose to the challenge, and developed a strong, robust organization. It was a challenging time for me too, as I gradually withdrew from its day to day work. I wanted to let the organization grow and develop without my being in charge, and I had to work hard to let that happen.

It is now one of the leading organizations in Ireland that work with housing and homelessness, providing housing, services and advocacy for thousands of people across the country. Focus Ireland has always been blessed with good, committed governance, in its chairpersons and non-executive and executive directors, and with great staff and volunteers. That continues to this day, under the direction of Gerry Danaher, Chairman, and Joyce Loughnan, CEO.

Although I have not been chief executive of Focus Ireland for many years now, I am life president of the organization and I am still involved with it in various ways, but much less intensely than in the past. One of the links I like to maintain is that I work one day a week in the coffee shop on Eustace Street, which was the very first piece of Focus Point when it was established in 1985. This is a nice way to maintain my connection to people who are out of home.

One reason I reduced my active involvement with Focus Ireland was that in 1997 I was elected to the General Leadership Team of the Congregation of the Religious Sisters of Charity. This meant that, along with the congregational leader and the rest of the team, I had responsibilities for the policy of the congregation and for overseeing its work throughout the world. This involved a good deal of travel in Ireland and Europe, as well as in North and South America and Africa. It was a very interesting time. It allowed me to experience many different cultures, ethnicities and faiths, and to see at first hand the ministries that the Sisters of Charity deliver throughout the world. I was inspired by so much that I saw. The sisters' ability to integrate with the local communities in the developing world, their commitment, dedication and sheer hard work, was quite amazing.

I also reduced my active involvement with Focus Ireland because I was very aware that Ireland was changing economically, socially and culturally, and new needs were emerging. I knew there were other projects I would have to pursue. And I thought about establishing an innovative organization that would respond to the emerging needs of the time.

8

Welcoming Change

In the year 2000, I was approached by a woman called Chantal McCabe. Chantal and her husband Liam had some funds available to them and wanted to contribute to a worthwhile project that would be something new in the light of our rapidly changing society. Chantal was looking for someone who had an overview of the social situation in Ireland and ideas for new responses to the needs. I told her about the ideas I had been developing, and she was very interested. And so it was that, with Chantal's support, I went about setting up a company called Social Innovations Ireland (SII).

I invited business people, including Chantal, to join the board of the new company. I have to say, looking back, that this was a real act of faith on the part of the people who came on board with me. I knew that Ireland was changing, and that new social needs would start to become apparent, but at that time I hadn't really clarified my thinking to the point where I could explain it in detail to other people. But they came with me, and together we formed SII, with the purpose of responding to new and emerging needs in

Ireland, whatever they might turn out to be. I was executive chairperson and we employed Geraldine Hegarty as general manager, and her assistant Nicole Rodger.

Very quickly new social needs began to emerge. Within a year, our thinking had moved on, and Social Innovations Ireland gave birth to two new projects, which were later (in 2004) to become companies in their own right: the Immigrant Council of Ireland (ICI) and the Young Social Innovators (YSI).

I felt from the start that there was a need in the area of immigration. We were a country that, throughout our history, had had experience of emigration, but during the boom times of the late 1990s and early 2000s, immigration was a totally new experience for us. Recent estimates put the number of immigrants in Ireland at about 550,000. Ireland is now a richly diverse country which has benefited economically, socially and culturally from the skills, life experiences, culture, different religions and perspectives brought to these shores by migrants. Emigration is now again a reality for many Irish people, but we have not simply reverted to being an emigration economy. Immigration also is a permanent and positive reality in this country, and we need to ensure Ireland has an integrated, transparent, rights-based immigration system and effective integration policies that reflect this reality.

Although I felt drawn to work with migrants, I was at first not quite certain what the nature of their need was, so I began by consulting with all the organizations and individuals that had an interest in immigration to Ireland. It quickly became clear that, while there were organizations working with asylum seekers and refugees, there was none responding to the increasing flows of immigrants to Ireland. Migrants were coming to work, study, visit, join family and/or set up businesses, rather than in search of asylum. It was, however, evident that there was a definite need for an organization to provide information, advice, legal aid and support to immigrants and their families, whose rights were minimal and also very unclear.

Having intuited this need, my next step was to establish an advisory group of people who had knowledge or experience of inward migration, and with that advisory group, we developed a strategic plan for what was to become the Immigrant Council of Ireland. This was in July 2001, and soon afterwards we started to implement our plan. John O'Donoghue was Minister for Justice at the time, and in December of that year he announced that he was providing funding of €150,000 for the Immigrant Council of Ireland in the 2002 budget. It was the first and last contribution we got from that department of government. By 2004, the Immigrant Council had been set up as an independent company with its own board.

In 2001 and 2002 we received funding from the Sisters of Charity. With that I was able to employ Hilkka Becker as a solicitor, and Fidèle Mutwarasibo as Policy and Information Advice Officer. We also had the part-time services of Geraldine Hegarty, who also worked with Young Social Innovators. This team set to work immediately on advice and legal help for those in need and set up a service of both high standard and good practice. In 2002 we also completed our *Labour Migrant Policy: a Handbook for Migrants*, the first information resource book on rights and entitlements of migrants. And the following year Taoiseach Bertie Ahern formally opened the service.

Later that year Denise Charlton was appointed chief executive. She continues in this post today, under the chairmanship of John Cunningham with the support of a hugely committed board of directors of which I am a member. It was under Denise's leadership that the scope of the work and the service offered broadened and deepened. Funded today by a major philanthropic organization and with some funding from the Religious Sisters of Charity, under Denise's leadership the Immigrant Council of Ireland has become a very strong, significant, vibrant and vocal NGO in the immigration sector.

Looking back on it now, although I went about setting up the ICI in a very different way from how I set up Focus Point in the 1980s, I can also see many similarities in my thinking and my practice. Just as I had been aware, all those years ago, that people's perception of homelessness among women was that it was almost non-existent (which turned out to be far from true), I could now see that people tended to think of immigration almost exclusively in terms of asylum. But I knew there was a whole other kind of migration that was scarcely recognized at the time. I suppose, partly because the arrival of asylum seekers was so sudden and new, and because for a considerable time it was the primary migration flow to Ireland, inevitably the perception was that people came to Ireland mainly for protection. In fact there was a time when the only way a non-EU migrant could get into Ireland was through the asylum system, and the public view was that we needed to protect ourselves as a country from an 'influx' of people flocking to our shores.

It is no coincidence that the immigration system was managed through the justice system, an indication that we saw migration as something from which we needed to protect ourselves. Even all these years on, there is still a tendency in the public mind to think of migrants as primarily refugees, and the immigration system is still handled through the justice system. Access to social goods such as education and healthcare continues to depend on the status a person has as an immigrant, as defined by the Department of Justice. In addition, much of the discourse from the state has been from Justice with its specific lens of state protection. It is a shame that other departments such as Education, Health, Enterprise and Tourism didn't join the public discourse, highlighting the continuous benefit to Ireland from migration in these core areas.

We in ICI were for some time the only people to think of immigration as an economic and social phenomenon. As the economy expanded and labour shortages became a problem, the government itself actually invited migrant workers to come to Ireland to take up the jobs we could not fill ourselves. But the people who came in response to our labour requirements, although they were welcome as units of labour, had very few entitlements. They were coming to fill a new economic need, but the legal and welfare infrastructure to meet *their* needs was not only non-existent – it hadn't even been thought about.

The Immigrant Council of Ireland was the first body to publicly frame the debate on migration, and gradually people began to understand what migration (as distinct from asylum-seeking) actually is. Our task as an organization representing migrants and their families has always been to try to understand and analyse migration flows and to work out the implications for infrastructure to support these flows. We try to establish why and how people come, what rights they have, issues relating to their families, access to services, and their legal rights of residence.

Our handbook for immigrants, as well as being a valuable information resource, was part of a redefinition of immigration. It was also a first attempt at what is a major part of our work with migrants: helping them to navigate the immigration system. From early on, we understood that information and access to legal rights were an overwhelming need for migrants. And that hasn't changed. It is still a big need, because the system is chaotic, unwieldy, bureaucratic and slow. We were not prepared for immigration in the first place; when it happened, we never caught up with all that needed to be done. Legislation that has been in the making for eight years is still not in place. We continue this work – constantly documenting how to navigate the system, and any changes – and share this resource with migrants directly but also with other NGOs and state agencies, through our service provision, resource materials and website.

A large part of ICI's strategy is to try to make the public and government aware of the context: to make it clear who comes, why they come and what their needs are. This is done primarily through research and publications. Our migration policy paper, *Labour Migration into Ireland* (2003), was the first time anyone set out information on the numbers of immigrants and why they are here. Now the Central Statistics Office provides information like this, and the Economic and Social Research Institute undertakes research, but for many years we were the only organization to do so. However, we continue to keep a record of evidence where there is a gap and a need to highlight emerging needs or issues. Examples include trafficking and prostitution, citizenship and residency, and pathways to homelessness for migrants. We hope to look at first- and second-generation migrant children in the future.

The ICI's information and referral service deals with over 10,000 enquiries from migrants and Irish citizens, and more than 250 organizations, each year. This interaction gives us a thorough understanding of the issues migrants are facing and informs our work in advocating for change.

Another crucial area of work is carried out by the legal team. The ICI is the only NGO in the immigration sector to have the status of 'independent law centre'. This was a crucial strategy for ICI. One of the few ways to effect change with regard to migration was through casework and litigation. Our approach aims to bring about change in public policy or in the law, its interpretation or its application – typically correcting a perceived injustice or achieving specific legislative, legal or other change. From early on, we recognized that, left to themselves, politicians wouldn't make change in the area of immigration, because it is not popular. But if politicians were reluctant to engage with the issue, going through the courts, we soon realized, is a way of bringing about change. In addition to litigation, through casework we are constantly working with the state to redefine policies and procedures for migrants, making small but significant changes to the system that result in better access to services for many migrants and their families.

The qualified solicitors who work for the ICI can provide legal representation to clients as well as doing important legal policy and lobbying work. Funding constraints mean that the ICI's legal service is limited. Cases are taken on when they are of strategic importance and may result in legislative or procedural change, or when the client is particularly vulnerable: for example, a victim of human rights abuses in Ireland such as exploitation as a victim of trafficking or of domestic violence; or someone who has particular health needs.

Intensive support is provided for vulnerable migrants through the specialist immigration advocacy service of ICI. Legal advice and other appropriate responses, such as referral of clients to additional service providers, is available through this service to women who have been trafficked into the country, women who have been subjected to sexual exploitation in the sex industry, victims of domestic violence, undocumented migrants and their families and unaccompanied minors.

Of equal importance to ensuring that migrants and their families are treated fairly in a transparent immigration system is the promotion of social, economic and cultural inclusion. For that reason, the ICI is deeply committed to ensuring that Ireland has effective integration policies. We have been involved in significant national and transnational projects aimed at identifying and over-coming barriers to effective integration. For example, the ICI recently ran a mentoring programme which brought together migrants with Irish or other long-established residents in a grass-roots integration project which will now be rolled out in communities around the country. We are presently working on a project within the school system, looking at migrant parental leadership in that context. At the European level, just one of the projects we are engaged in with transnational partners involves identifying and overcoming barriers young migrants face in maximizing their career potential.

We have undertaken groundbreaking research on issues of fundamental importance in this area, such as English-language provision, the feminization of migration and the need for a holistic approach to meeting migrants' needs, as well as research comparing the integration experiences of specific nationality groups in Ireland.

A major influence on the experiences of migrants in Ireland now, as we enter a new decade, is the economic crisis facing Ireland. Although the recession has had a devastating impact on the entire country, evidence has emerged that unemployment has disproportionately affected migrants. This is reflected in the live register and also in the types of enquiries the ICI receives from migrants, and is starkly evident in the increased number of homeless migrants. The downturn has given an added impetus to the need to ensure that debate about immigration and integration in the broader context of a commitment to social justice is fair, factual and balanced.

At the ICI, we put considerable effort into communicating what we learn from migrants through the information and referral service, the legal casework, our policy development and integration projects. By providing evidence-based commentary, we reveal migrants' experiences in this country and the necessity for reform. It is not enough simply to identify what is wrong with the system: it is crucial to formulate proposals for workable solutions. Bringing a human-rights-based approach to public discourse on immigration and integration is critically important, particularly in times of economic crisis, if our communities are to enjoy social cohesion in the future.

ICI sees its work as being all about interconnection. We need to make a connection between the debate on how immigration is perceived and the actual impact of immigration. This in turn has a real effect on policies and laws regarding who can migrate and how, and in turn this influences the debate. We set out to understand the problem, using evidence-based research, so that we can then communicate that perception of the problem, and this provides the arguments we need if we are to insist upon reforms.

Individual experience is very important in what ICI is trying to do. We are constantly thinking about the appropriate response to the individual; then we take that response and try to improve the system that caused the problem for the individual in the first place. In our way of thinking and working, policy is practice and practice influences policy – they are closely interlinked. People often say that we should make up our mind about the kind of organization we are – we should be lobbyists or a think tank or a service provider – but that is not how we work. We prefer to participate at all levels, and one area of work informs another. Our experience with individuals and their problems gives us evidence of what the problem is so that we can try to find solutions. We try to use individual experience to indicate a general need or a problem in the system that can then be addressed through policy and legislation.

The situation changes all the time, and reflection plays an

important role. In fact, it is built into the organization. This is something I know from my own experience. I am constantly pushing people in the organization to think about what the problems are and what kinds of methods will help us to arrive at a solution.

In recent times, new issues have emerged. For example, second-generation migrants have different problems from their parents. The popular idea is that most immigrants have already gone home, but that's not true. The second-generation migrants are challenging us to think about who is Irish and what it means to be Irish: who belongs here? As well as new problems, the initial difficulties that were in the immigration system are still there and still relevant.

Racism is starting to become a huge problem in Ireland. Prejudice is based on factors such as skin colour, faith and country of origin. There is even prejudice that relates to how people came to the state: there can be more prejudice against asylum seekers than there is against economic migrants, probably because asylum seekers are often from other continents and are seen as more different; economic migrants are more likely to be from mainland Europe, more likely to be like us.

Even though the state officially welcomed migrant workers coming to meet needs in the labour market, it has always regarded migration as a temporary measure, a labour strategy. For this reason, wc have never really taken on board the fact that Ireland is now a multicultural society.

Since the economic downturn, there have naturally been changes in the migrant population. Those who have come the furthest,

GLOBALISATION,
SEX TRAFFICKING
ND PROSTITUTION:

THE EXPERIENCES
MIGRANT WOMEN IN IRELAND

The Sisters of Charity funded the groundbreaking research project on the trafficking of women and children for sexual exploitation, which was carried out by the ICI. Today they continue to fund legal services for women who have been trafficked. (*Irish Times*) especially people from Africa, have the most to lose by leaving Ireland, and so they tend to stay. Europeans are much more flexible, and they have access to other labour markets, so they have tended to leave in greater numbers since the economy began to experience difficulties.

ICI views the immigration scene through a certain type of lens. We think in terms of the vulnerability of migrant populations and especially in terms of human rights violations. We maintain a special focus on women and girls who have been recruited into the sex industry. The support of the Sisters of Charity has been crucial in this work. I have pointed out to the Sisters of Charity how our work in the ICI, on behalf of women at risk and who have no voice, is in the direct tradition of Mary Aikenhead, and relates closely to the work I did all those years ago in trying to serve the needs of women out of home.

The Sisters of Charity funded our research in 2008 on trafficking of women and children for the purposes of sexual exploitation. This was groundbreaking research, the first major piece of research in the area, and it made Ireland realize for the first time that there was an issue here. As a result of this research, the state went from denial to accepting that there was a problem. The Sisters of Charity now fund the ICI legal services for women who have been trafficked. Since 2008, the ICI has been able to work with others to progress greater provision of services and protection for women and girls exploited in the sex industry. Through an EU-funded project, with Dublin Employment Pact, we were able to bring together NGOs and state providers, national and international, to consider the best service provision for victims. There is still a long way to go: at present we convene an NGO alliance of groups to continue to lobby and call for greater protection and high-quality services for victims. We also convene a coalition of groups that advocate a legislative change to tackle demand for the purchase of sex. There is increasing support for this and we are hopeful that a new government will support this important change to protect vulnerable women and girls from exploitation within the sex industry.

Again like Focus, we communicate the change priorities we are advocating. Both organizations use strategies that include major conferences and strategic dialogue/seminars to highlight issues. We always have the best speakers at our conferences, people from outside the country who have had a lot of experience. Both national and international experts frame the debate and comment on the situation. In this way, we can influence policy.

Our conferences and public discussions focus on identifying emerging needs. In 2011, for example, our theme was young people and their experience of immigration. We used focus groups to get them to express what the experience has been like for them.

The permission that was given to migrants during the boom period, when there were jobs to be filled, is being withdrawn, now that we are in recession. But recession or no recession, the fact is that we now have an immigrant population, many of whom have chosen to remain in this country. But we still haven't accepted that our population is different now and will stay different: different faiths, nationalities, cultures – children growing up with different experiences. And it is that range of experience that ICI continues to seek to address.

9

Education for Active Citizenship

Everywhere these days there is fear, anger and distrust. Our financial system has disintegrated around us, our leaders have failed us, even our Church has let us down badly. Our sense of security is mortally shaken, and the public are set on blame, scapegoating and vengeance. We are in the gutter, no doubt about it, but, as Wilde says, at least we are looking at the stars.

The bright firmament of our democracy may seem rather dim to people who have lost their jobs or are living in fear of losing them, or to those who have lost their houses or their savings, and I do not for one moment make light of the serious plight of so many hard-working people who see their life's work coming to nothing; nevertheless, we have a unique opportunity now to rebuild our whole social system from the bottom up, not on the model of the cappuccino culture of the marketplace, to which we have for so long been in thrall, but on sound democratic principles.

'Democracy,' says Václav Havel, 'is a system based on trust in human responsibility. This responsibility, however, must be constantly nurtured and cultivated. The State . . . should trust its citizens and enable them to share in a substantive way the exercise of responsibility for the condition of society.'

Our concept of citizenship has evolved over time. Though the Ancient Greeks had an early form of democracy, it was not until the eighteenth century that we developed the concept of the free, autonomous human being with rights enshrined in charters and constitutions, a concept that underlies our current view: that individuals are essentially social beings and that the cultural community into which we are born shapes our identity and sense of self. There is a new recognition today that the concept of citizen must allow for the inclusion of different cultural identities.

In Ireland, the concept of 'Irish citizenship' has also evolved. As author and academic Wendy Ross has pointed out, our sense of 'active democratic citizenship' now relies more on loyalty to democratic institutions than on an identity based on birth, language or religion. This kind of 'civic republicanism' requires a balance between rights and duties, and it emphasizes the active participation of the citizen in both political and social life with a sense of common citizenship in a modern, diverse Ireland. This wider concept of Irish citizenship, with its potential for inclusiveness, is a welcome development, but it does not go far enough, since it does not extend to the connectedness and care for each other that Havel places at the heart of his concept of democracy.

When we practise citizenship as human connectedness, our commitment to caring for others is neither a burdensome duty nor a token in some kind of elaborate social exchange: it is for the sake of the relationship itself. When citizens are connected, they do the kinds of things we would wish good citizens to do: they vote, they volunteer, they participate. But that's not the point, or it is only part of the point. Citizens who have this kind of human connect-edness have confidence in themselves, a sense of belonging and of being needed and valued. As the poet Brendan Kennelly so simply puts this in his poem 'Connection', 'self knows that self is not enough'. Self connected to others is what we are about.

Citizenship as human connectedness is not some kind of mushy, feel-good idea: it is about real engagement, and the opening of hearts and minds. As Havel points out, we can only have this kind of democracy if we educate our young people for it. In her plea for a major intervention on social and political education, Kathleen Lynch of UCD argues that young people need skills in critical think-ing, in research and analysis, in understanding the assumptions and concepts embedded in the systems and structures of society: 'One cannot provide love or connection on a rational basis,' she says, 'or easily measure its outcomes in quantifiable terms.' Nevertheless, 'civic competencies' can be encouraged, taught and valued in our schools and colleges so that we are nurturing and cultivating 'trust in human responsibility' and citizens with open minds and open hearts, who care for each other and for the democratic institutions, charters and constitutions that sustain them.

The Crick Report: *Education for Citizenship and the Teaching of Democracy in Schools* (London, QCA, 1998) provides one definition of citizenship education:

We aim at no less than a change in the political culture of this country both nationally and locally: for people to think of themselves as active citizens, willing, able and equipped to have an influence in public life and with the critical capacities to weigh evidence before speaking and acting; to build on and to extend radically to young people the best in existing traditions of community involvement and public service, and make them individually confident in finding new forms of involvement and action among themselves.

In Ireland, Civic, Social and Political Education is a compulsory subject at the junior cycle of secondary school. It aims to prepare students for active participatory citizenship. This is achieved through comprehensive exploration of their lives at a time when pupils are developing from children into independent young adults. It should produce knowledgeable pupils who can explore, analyse and evaluate, who are skilled and practised in moral and critical appraisal, and capable of making decisions and judgements through a reflective citizenship, based on human rights and social responsibilities.

But education for responsible citizenship cannot be allowed to end at the age of 15, and indeed it is hoped that Civic, Social and Political Education will soon be available at senior cycle. This is a welcome development, but I would urge educators to ensure that the programme includes action. It is essential that such a subject has action as an integral part of the programme, and by action I do not mean just undertaking project work. Citizenship as connectedness is not something that can be taught. It can only be learned, and it must be learned through experience and active engagement with real communities, by undertaking research into actual social issues and coming up with and implementing solutions in the communities themselves.

And that is why a programme such as the Young Social Innovators (YSI) is so important. Around the same time, in 2001, that ICI was becoming a major activity of Social Innovations Ireland, Young Social Innovators was also starting to develop. The idea of developing and supporting young social innovators emerged initially out of a discussion I had with Rachel Collier. Rachel worked with me in Focus Point/Focus Ireland, and we were both very aware of the contribution that young people could make to society, and the lack of opportunities and structures to enable that contribution, especially at second-level education.

I took up the idea with the board of Social Innovations Ireland (SII) who agreed to fund the YSI as a pilot project. The main thrust of Young Social Innovators was to create programmes of social and community awareness that would operate in second-level schools around the country. Rachel was employed by SII to develop the pilot project, with the assistance of Geraldine Hegarty and Nicole Rodger. The pilot was a huge success. Rachel has continued since then in YSI as its chief executive, to lead its growth and development as a strong and vibrant national organization in the area of active innovative citizenship. In 2004 YSI became a company in its own right, well run by a very committed board of directors, of which I am chairperson, and YSI still strives to provide just the kind of caring and active citizenship that Havel talks about.

Education was a new area for Rachel and me, and our approach was to bring our previous experience of social innovation over the

In Aras an Uachtaran with President Mary McAleese and the
YSI Award winners, 2009. (Photo by Derek Speirs)

years to bear on this new venture. The critical point in social innovation, as the development of Focus Point exemplified, is the movement from passion and ideas to action.

The YSI programme started in Dublin with a small number of schools in 2001. The following year Young Social Innovators extended to Leinster and then to Leinster/Munster, and for the past five years it has been a nationwide programme. Between 2002 and 2010, more than 30,000 young people have been involved in YSI projects. In 2010 alone there were over 6,000 young people participating.

YSI's mission is to 'fire young people's passion to change the world for good'. Initially slotting in at Transition Year at second level, and now extending to all 15–18-year-olds, the programme is designed to empower young people to explore being part of a society and see how their actions can have a real impact on others' lives. It was designed so that the young people who participate in it discover that they can make a difference and that they are connected to the communities they are part of.

The philosophy underlying Young Social Innovators consists of four key elements: caring, co-operation, communication and change, and in all these areas we drew on our Focus experience.

To take caring first, a central value of Focus Point was responding to the need, as it was with YSI. This core value means that the young people involved in identifying a social issue they wish to become active in need to care passionately about that issue, whatever it may be. The fire of empathy can only be fuelled if they care deeply and are moved to respond to the problem.

The value of co-operation and teamwork was also very much

part of Focus Point. Working in partnership with existing bodies and interested people multiplies the effect that a social innovation can have. There are few issues that don't have other interested people/bodies trying to make a difference. Joining forces often leads to more effective action.

Since its foundation, Focus Point drew on the collective experience of the people involved. By co-operating actively with existing services at home and abroad, Focus Point was able to have a wider impact on both policies and practices. Similarly, co-operation and teamwork became an integral part of the YSI programme.

By definition, social innovation is about doing something new, and new ideas need to be communicated and explained to a wider audience. New understandings need to be created through effective communication of those ideas, and a new language may need to be developed to describe them. For this reason, effective communication is a central part of social innovation and we have made it an essential element of the YSI programme. Clarity of message is important, as is the ability to select and use appropriate media to communicate that message.

Again, this was learned from Focus Point's experience. One of the greatest challenges facing Focus Point from the beginning was communicating ideas about homelessness. Homelessness was stigmatized, and it required work to combat the negative stereotype that was so prevalent, and to some extent still is.

The negative ideas people had tended to affect their perception of homeless people, which was not helpful when it came to garnering support for our work. And so Focus Point set out to change that perception and to some extent to create new ideas and a new language in the public discussion of homelessness.

This was achieved through communicating the idea that homelessness can happen to almost anyone, given certain personal and social circumstances.

One major change was to use the language that people out of home used themselves to describe their situation, and this change in the way homelessness was talked about helped to change attitudes and thinking about homelessness, an effect that is still obvious today in the language of policy-makers and activists in the field. Most importantly, the voice of people out of home was heard, and this empowerment, as well as creating relevant solutions to their issues, was inspiring and now influences the thinking behind and approach of YSI.

Social innovation is about creating change: change in how we think, feel and care for other people, and change that is active, relevant and new. Everyone can create change; everyone can make a difference; and there is a role and responsibility for every person to innovate for the benefit of all. As humans we are creative imaginers, and we can make change happen because we have the imagination and the vision and the foresight that shape change. The experience of knowing this can have a profound impact on personal development.

In YSI, learning about change is integral to learning about social innovation. Those affected by change are often the best promoters of that change. Their influence on how and what change happens is enormous. However, change is not always good and change that does not emerge from a thorough understanding of a problem and empathy with a need can be misguided and even irrelevant.

YSI offers young people the opportunity to research and take action on a social issue that they themselves identify. Young people are its heart, and young participants need to guide the future of YSI. Just as people out of home helped to establish Focus Point, so YSI is youth-led in its activities.

Working in teams, YSI participants explore their chosen issue, decide on an action they can take to effect change, and follow through on that.

In summary, YSI projects have to have certain key elements or principles:

- Be youth-led – the young people themselves pick the topic they work on.
- Be based on teamwork and building partnerships.
- Involve reaching a high level of understanding – so that the participants understand the 'why' as well as the 'what' of their chosen issue.
- Be action-driven – some change has to be effected and the results communicated to the wider community.

YSI offers training for the teachers who facilitate the work and a range of innovative material in print and on the web. Local and national platforms such as 'Speak Outs' and the annual YSI Showcase ensure that young people's voices are heard; and celebration of the young people's achievements in effecting change has always been an integral part of the programme – active citizens need recognition for their work. High visibility of their actions is achieved with the help of a supportive local and national media.

Working with education and community partners, YSI also provides new opportunities to link the school to the local community, business groups and national institutions. In the very way YSI works, it builds trust and connectedness from the ground up.

Consider a group of students who want to tackle poverty in the world. That's their starting point. What does the teacher do in the YSI class? Rather than toning down their ambitions, she draws their ideas out, gets them to examine the aspects they feel strongly about, distils these, and helps them use imaging techniques to see what they can achieve. And so their journey begins, they build a team and roles are identified, plans made and put into action. The YSI Award title holders recently from Coláiste Bhríde Carnew and St Peter's College Dunboyne did just this, and not only in one classroom: they linked together and formed a large collective of young people working on a very challenging project.

Their work introduced them to all sorts of new partners including Self Help Africa, Irish Aid, National University of Ireland, Maynooth and others along the way who were only too glad to link in and help out in any way they could. The power of this collective was strong. Their ambitions in the end were manifested in creating and hosting a Poverty Week in the schools, which involved students and teachers living in poverty. They created a guide so that this could be replicated in other schools and there are plans to distribute it to all schools. They wanted to create awareness of the first Millennium Development Goal, to eradicate poverty and hunger, and so wrote to hundreds of people to ask about their views on poverty. This resulted in a high-quality, well-designed book called *Twenty Fifteen*.

I give this example of a YSI project to demonstrate how it actually works – fostering the youth-led initiative; building partners; exploring and learning more about the issue; communicating and creating new actions and working together as a team to maximize effort and effect. It is active citizenship – and it is powerful in action. When done well, it demonstrates to all concerned that we are all connected and can make a big difference to the world.

The frameworks and models developed by YSI for their programmes are founded on – and contribute to – best practice in citizenship education as identified in the 2008 European Study of Active Citizenship Education. Any successful programme, this study found, had to have the key components that are in fact the cornerstones of the YSI approach.

Citizenship education has to be concerned with relationships between individuals and their community; be underpinned by democratic values; have the active participation of students and young people; and ensure that young people develop the knowledge, attitudes and skills to participate fully in public and community life.

Our system claims to aspire to develop people who are 'civic-minded, responsible and creative', but the system itself often militates against this possibility. Researchers from the University of Limerick, who carried out an evaluation of the impact of YSI in 2008, found that the school system itself can be a hostile environment for programmes such as YSI. This, the researchers suggest – basing their views on detailed work carried out by the OECD on our school system in 1991– is because our second-level schools still operate a static, subject-based curriculum, with 'instruction dominated' forms of teaching, text-based learning and competitive assessment through examinations: the traditional academic 'transmission model of teaching', with the stress on 'systems and structures rather than beliefs and values'.

There is a new emphasis and even rhetoric on developing students who are ready for a future 'smart economy'. This opens up possibilities for our future economic prosperity. Concentration on a goal like this should not be at the expense of an education that helps people to feel connected to and responsible for each other. It is smarter, I think, to develop a society which promotes economic, social, environmental and cultural prosperity equally. These coexist and our smartness in one should be linked intrinsically to smartness in another. This is the 'smart' way to be and to live.

There are many programmes for young people with very worthy aims: to reduce teenage pregnancy, for example, or to stop antisocial behaviour or curtail drug use. Such programmes may have good effects, but it is far more beneficial in the long run to convince young people that they matter. And the way to do this is to provide them with opportunities to connect and to act to change the world. This is a challenge to our system, and giving them real opportunities to do this is about trusting people, as Havel says. It is about believing that young people will take responsibility for their own actions. That is what is at the heart of the YSI programme. In itself, the organization is a living example of active

141

citizenship and social innovation. Over the years, young people taking part in the programme have researched and taken action on such thorny issues as bullying in schools, child trafficking, homelessness, drug misuse, the plight of immigrants, body image, attitudes to Travellers and other minority groups, to name but a few of the projects that come to mind. They have demonstrated not only that they understand the issues involved, but that they can, through their actions, 'change the world for good'.

YSI has developed its thinking and is now working in a more holistic way, encouraging social action across the whole school. A two-year pilot programme in selected schools is exploring opportunities for social awareness education on a whole-school basis and is motivating more young people to get involved in projects that help their communities. The ultimate aim of the pilot is to have new frameworks and new models in place which can work within the school system and, in so doing, really encourage that system so that it is developing, nurturing and cultivating young, active citizens in everything it does. It is an ambitious aim, undertaken with scarce resources, but with creativity, hard work, a passion for social justice and the mobilization of the goodwill of committed school principals, teachers and young social advocates and innovators in the school system as well as willing partners in the state, voluntary and business sectors.

At third level too, we need to engage our young people in active citizenship programmes. There are some fine examples of these developing. They do not need to be part of the formal, examined curriculum, but should be integrated into the lives of students – in the way sports are, for example, at the moment – so that our brightest and most innovative young people who will go on to become the leaders and opinion-formers of our society can engage in social issues at a time in their lives when they have energy and enthusiasm. They can then bring the skills, experiences and attitudes formed by such engagement into their professional lives. We might well look to US colleges for models in this regard.

These are testing times for Ireland and the world. We are now discovering that trust is the basis of our economic system as it is the basis of our political and social systems. When trust goes, the very foundation of our democracy is in peril. Our deepest yearning as human beings is to be valued and loved. Love is not created by legal charters and constitutions, vital though these are, but grows out of our relationships and connections. If we want to change our reality, then we have to have the social tools to do that – a way of listening to each other, talking to each other, connecting to each other, trusting each other.

Our challenge now is to encourage young people to maintain their natural generosity of spirit and concern for others as they journey to adulthood. We learn by doing and by the response we receive from our peers and our communities, and so the practical experience of doing citizenship is essential. By providing such opportunities through education programmes like Young Social Innovators, we are nurturing and cultivating the new citizens of tomorrow, trusting that they know better than us how to change the world for good. All we have to do is to fire their passion and imagination and give them the social tools to learn to become, in Seamus Heaney's phrase, 'dual citizens' – citizens of their country and citizens of the 'Republic of Conscience'.

10

The Marginalization of Dissent

Back in the 1970s when I was chair of the Committee on Pilot Schemes to Combat Poverty, I encountered government resistance, and I was in effect threatened with 'consequences' if I continued to criticize government policy. As described in Chapter 4, I suspect that my refusal to capitulate to this kind of subtle bullying was at least partly to blame for the government's withdrawal of funds from projects I was involved in.

Some people might say that I was misguided in sticking to my guns and refusing to keep quiet about what I saw as faulty policies. Shouldn't organizations, particularly those in receipt of public money, just get on with the job, this argument goes, without being seen to be 'politicking'? There are two points I would make in response to that kind of thinking.

Firstly, tolerance of dissent is crucial in a modern democracy. Organizations whose remit involves speaking out with or on behalf of the disadvantaged or marginalized are charged with seeking to change society, to make it fairer and to remove obstacles to achieving a just society. All the evidence suggests that where there is misinformation or stereotyping of groups who are disadvantaged, poor or perceived as 'other', society will make it harder to express dissent. It is a particularly difficult task for groups such as Travellers, prisoners, drug users, people with mental health needs, asylum seekers or migrants.

Where prejudice, misinformation and stereotyping exist, marginalization is exacerbated. Civic dialogue between such groups and society's dominant stakeholders is important if the rights and responsibilities of individuals are to be explored and understood. This civic dialogue should be a two-way process. Public discourse and dialogue between such groups is essential in any society so that its citizens are informed, so that the different interest groups' perceptions of each other are changed and new public policies can be developed to better respond to changing circumstances. At times, considered criticisms of the status quo must inevitably be made. If we fail to criticize we fail those whose position at the margins of our society means their voices are not otherwise heard.

Secondly, when intolerance of criticism extends to an unwillingness to listen to suggestions for a better society, or a fairer way of doing government business or providing services, then the consequences are real and can be severe. The result may be the promotion of mediocrity – the perception that even obviously faulty ways of doing business are 'fine' the way they are. At the extreme end of the spectrum, the scandalous can be allowed to occur without actually causing scandal. In some circumstances, the result can be denial of access to justice.

Since 1980, we have witnessed significant changes in how the state engages with the community and voluntary sector, as well as legislative changes regarding the promotion of human rights and access to information held by state agencies. The community and voluntary sector is now an accepted partner in the social framework, which allows the promotion of social policy issues to be expressed within that framework. The state has committed to investment in some areas such as social housing provision and the financing of services for people with disabilities. The critical issue now is whether these commitments will be honoured. A key question for the voluntary sector is: to what degree does it enjoy influence within this process and are its voice and independence being reduced as a result of its involvement?

Intolerance of dissent did not stop in the 1970s, and in my work I see many examples of government attempts to manipulate people who work for voluntary organizations and try to champion the cause of those who are disadvantaged and marginalized.

In 2000, the Irish government published a *White Paper on a Framework for Supporting Voluntary Activity and for Developing the Relationship between the State and the Community and Voluntary Sector*. It included, as one of its key principles, that the state and the voluntary sector each recognize their 'mutual right to constructively critique each other's actions and policies'. However, the process of implementing the White Paper's recommendations was stymied and the group charged with this responsibility was disbanded in 2007.

To me, the marginalization of dissent is most apparent in the weakness of the voices expressing dissent, and this weakness is a direct result of the pressure brought to bear on voluntary bodies which must negotiate with the state with regard to the planning and funding of their services.

There are many examples of how our society has improved for the benefit of many as a direct result of campaigning by groups and individuals who were brave enough to say that the status quo is not good enough and who advocated for a better, more efficient or fairer way forward. One of the most recent involves the treatment of people with cystic fibrosis.

There is, however, a worryingly wide range of methods used in Irish society to stifle the voices of those who advocate on behalf of the marginalized. In the first place, there is legislation such as the Charities Act. This Act precludes new organizations, which state that one of their aims is to advocate in relation to human rights, from being registered as a charity.

Another strategy is to cut funding to organizations that cause embarrassment or discomfiture or that challenge the status quo. Sometimes clauses are included in funding contracts – or employment contracts – which prevent the organization in question, or specific individuals, from speaking out. State-funded organizations are required to seek clearance for press releases or publications from government departments before they are released. This, along with other measures such as the use of anonymous 'official sources' to discredit the work of NGOs in the media, creates and fosters a prevailing perception that dissenting views are unwelcome or, at worst, disadvantageous for an NGO's client base.

Some of these measures are deliberate government policy decisions, but others rely on the help, willing or otherwise, of

'Count Us In' – an ICI campaign (2011) to raise awareness of the problems facing migrants who have become Irish citizens, and who have a vote. (Photo by Marc O'Sullivan)

others to be effective – the media or even the NGOs themselves. This is not a sign of freely accepting a muzzle, but of the very difficult and stark choices that sometimes must be made.

Transparency – meaning both openness and accountability – is key to promoting a civic society and enabling dissent. This principle applies to state bodies, the churches and the community voluntary sector. The NGO sector needs to be more transparent regarding its finances and work practices. We should not be afraid of critical comment if it is informed. We need new structures and systems and models of development to enable dissent in Ireland.

Key factors in enabling dissent are good governance and an open government. Proper financing and broadening the remit for equality infrastructure – the Human Rights Commission, the Equality Authority and the Ombudsman's Office, for example – and ending the restrictions in the Freedom of Information Act would be good indicators of a commitment to openness. And a questioning media has a central role to play.

11

A Vision of Social Justice for the Ireland of the Future

Imagine a child born into the Ireland of tomorrow. It could be your child or grandchild; it might be a child born into a struggling inner-city family or a middle-class suburban family, into an immigrant family or a Traveller family, in a town or a city or in rural Ireland; it might be a girl or a boy; it might be born into a two-parent family, or it might be the child of a single mother; it might be a healthy child, or a child born with HIV or with a disability; it might be born into poverty or into comfort; it might be a little Muslim or a little Catholic or the child of secular parents; its mother tongue might be English or Irish, Polish or French or Arabic.

Whatever its family background, genetic heritage, cultural identity or health status, it is easy to recognize and natural to want to respond to the vulnerability and myriad needs of a new baby: the need for love and security, safety and warmth, food and shelter. Surely we can agree that all our children should be able to grow up free of violence, oppression and addiction, to be safe from trafficking, slavery and exploitation, and to have their health, housing, educational and economic needs met, as of right. If we can agree that this is what we want for every child in the country, then we have already signed up to the principles underlying social justice. A society that is built on social justice is a society that provides for all its citizens according to their needs.

But somehow, it doesn't work like that. Even if we acknowledge the desirability of this ideal, we don't seem to be able to work it out in practice. The problem is that our society is deeply divided along economic, social, religious, cultural and ethnic lines. These divisions are deeply embedded in our experience and they control our opportunities. And yet, we only acquire commitment to these divisions as we grow into our culture, and they are totally irrelevant in the face of the needs of the helpless newborn.

If we can keep that image of the newborn child with all its vulnerability and dependency in front of us, perhaps we can dream up ways of re-envisaging our society so that every newborn in this country is safe and warm and fed and sheltered and can grow up as a literate, thinking citizen with real and realizable opportunities to participate in the social, economic, educational, artistic, spiritual, sporting and civic life of the country.

The most blatant manifestation of social injustice is poverty, and we will never have social justice while we have people living in poverty in this country. Even when this society was at its richest, before the end of the twentieth century, 10 per cent of our children lived in 'consistent poverty'. We might think of consistent poverty as dire poverty; in essence, not having enough money to supply even the most basic needs for food and warmth. We had a national plan to eradicate consistent poverty by the year 2016, but it seems unlikely now that we will meet this target.

The poverty I witnessed as a child was seeing individuals – children – who had less than others. And there was a distinction between those who owned something, like a farm or a shop, and those who didn't. The poverty I experienced after I joined the Sisters of Charity involved small sections of the community where there was unemployment and lack of basic resources like food and clothing. Today, it seems that poverty goes hand in hand with alienation and the marginalization of sections of the population.

There appears to be a much wider gap between the rich and the poor – and more blatant manifestations of wealth, which marginalizes the poor. Poverty is never easy – and it can be nasty. It is much harder to cope with when one is surrounded by wealth and plenty.

But if poverty itself is a serious barrier to social justice, the refusal by the well-off to believe in the existence of poverty is perhaps even more serious. And worse again than a refusal to accept that we have poverty in our country is a grudging acknowledgement of its existence accompanied by a 'blame' mentality that says poor people are poor because they are lazy or stupid or drink too much. Lots of rich people are lazy or stupid or drink too much, but nobody ever seems to make a connection between those personal shortcomings and their economic status.

The myth that people choose poverty or somehow deserve their poverty is the most insidious myth in our society. People are poor by and large because they are born poor, just as people are generally rich because they are born rich or they are born into a family with sufficient means to allow them to become rich. Of course there is some social mobility in our society, and people may acquire funds and status through a combination of talent, hard work and good luck over time, usually several generations, but really poor people rarely become really rich.

One reason for this is that being really poor is a full-time job in itself; when people are poor the odds are stacked against them. All their energy is used trying to make ends meet. Everything is difficult. If you have money to provide food on the table, life is much simpler. If you are rich and you want to keep warm, it is easy. If you are living in a cold, damp house, it is a never-ending battle to keep warm. It is also so much more difficult to access social welfare and health services. It takes time, it takes energy, and one's entire day revolves around basic survival.

Although poverty is defined largely in economic terms, it has complex effects in every area of the life of the poor – effects like social exclusion, high educational drop-out rates and poor mental and physical health – that make it almost impossible to move out of poverty. A life of poverty is such a life of entrapment that people can only move out of poverty if society decides that poverty is unacceptable and chooses to eradicate it and the social evils that go with it, and give people of every income level the opportunity to participate fully in the life of the nation.

Even if we do eradicate 'consistent poverty', we still have a very long way to go before we have a socially just society. Twenty per cent of our population are living on survival incomes – just enough to feed the family from week to week and pay the bills, but not enough to sustain the kind of life that most of us, even those of us who do not think of ourselves as well-off, consider normal. This 'relative' poverty does not even figure in the government's thinking when it comes to eradicating poverty, but people living on very low incomes, whether they are in low-paid jobs or on social welfare, also suffer the real effects of poverty: they are unable to make the kinds of choices about what they eat or where they live that the rest of us take for granted and they suffer social exclusion and disempowerment, as well as poor health and educational prospects. Over time, not being able to afford more than the absolute basics of life erodes the ability to cope and almost inevitably people in this situation will eventually come up against a problem that they cannot solve because of their economic situation: a serious illness, for example, or loss of a job. For the average person, such an event can be traumatic, but for a poor family, it can be the beginning of a total breakdown of family life and lead to debt, mental illness, addiction or homelessness. But because they are not in the very severest category of consistent poverty, they do not even figure in our national consciousness as being in need of having their issues addressed. We have to change our thinking as a society and acknowledge that poverty cannot be measured in absolute terms; nor can a notional amount of money be identified as sufficient. What people need is not some arbitrary income. What they need is enough to live on. In other words, if we are to eradicate the grinding effects of poverty, we have to start by meeting people's actual needs.

As long as we do not see the meeting of people's needs as the basis for an equitable civic society, we will continue to have babies who at birth are already severely disadvantaged by their family circumstances. Their parents could be ill or impoverished, addicted or separated from family members by immigration restrictions, or they may just be struggling to meet their financial commitments. Babies born into families in certain areas of our major cities are very likely to grow up with an array of problems associated with poverty: the child may go hungry on occasions and be cold in winter; or may not be able to play safely in their own neighbourhood, if there are problems of crime and drugs; the family might find it difficult to send the child to school every day, properly dressed and equipped. Inevitably the depressed and intimidating environment of our country's most run-down housing estates, possibly with gangland violence outside the front door – combined with multi-generational unemployment, poor educational attainment, inadequate housing and poor nutrition – will prescribe a life of multiple deprivation, early school-leaving, unemployment and possibly crime, prostitution and imprisonment. All of this surrounds a child born into that environment, as surely as a child born on the other side of town into a privileged family is likely to get a leaving certificate, possibly a degree and a well-paid job.

My vision for the Ireland of tomorrow is of a place where such predictions cannot so confidently be made about a child as it comes into the world. Rather it should be a place where any parents of a newborn baby can be sure that the needs of their child will be met. It should not be relevant whether they themselves are well-off, employed, healthy and well supported by family, friends and neighbours, or whether they are themselves young and vulnerable, have health issues or a disability, have experienced poverty or homelessness in their lives. Ideally, any baby born in our country will have equal and unquestioned access to the services and help it needs: access to suitable housing in a safe environment with appropriate facilities; quick and easy access to the healthcare that it needs, regardless of its parents' income; easy and unquestioned access to suitable education, from preschool onwards, especially if the child has particular educational needs – without its parents having to fight and plead and take court cases about it.

Needs-based housing, health and education provision is the cornerstone of social justice and the least we should expect of a society that calls itself Christian, humane, modern and democratic. In theory, we already subscribe to that ideal, but in practice we have not got it right. We have virtually stopped providing local authority housing and in recent years have relied heavily on largely profit-motivated landlords to provide accommodation for homeless families, and we allowed profit-driven developers to make our planning and building decisions, instead of properly qualified and disinterested planners. Our health service is notoriously two-tier, with long queues and waiting lists in the public system and virtually instant access for private patients, and our provision for people with psychiatric illnesses is appalling. Our free education system is in fact very expensive to participate in, especially at second and third level. If we are to have a society built on social justice, we need not only to take major steps towards eradicating poverty, but to radically restructure our provision of the basic services of health, education and housing, so that every child born in the Ireland of tomorrow is adequately provided for, as of right.

Imagine now that our national baby, so to speak, is growing up. This baby ideally lives with its family in a warm and adequately spacious home in a healthy environment and a safe neighbourhood that is free of guns, drugs and crime, with green spaces and places to play, well served by local shops and facilities and good public transport. Ideally the child's parents are supported by grandparents and extended family, and the child grows up in a mixed community and forms good and safe relationships with family members, older people, family friends and other children.

The abuse of children that has taken place in the past, and is doubtless still going on in families and institutions, has left a terrible wound in our society that may take generations to heal. One sad consequence is that children today have to be taught to be distrustful of adults, and that adults are afraid of forming friendships with children. As ways are found of detecting and treating paedophiliac tendencies in adults and offenders are quickly removed from the company of children, I hope that the children of the future, guided by safe and loving adults, can form good and appropriate relationships with people of all ages in their communities. In working our way through the complex of problems of child abuse that has come to light in recent years, we need to establish new ways of keeping our children safe without losing respectful adult–child contact and without permanently alienating adults of goodwill from all areas of contact with children. A sad repercussion of our understandable caution about adult–child relationships has been the falling away of adults who were once willing to volunteer to work with children in areas like sports and youth clubs. This is a serious loss to children and families, as well as opening up a gap that society has not yet found ways of filling. We need to find new ways of encouraging people to volunteer, not only in youth work but in all areas of life, if we are not to lose that spirit of selflessness, solidarity and community that volunteering means.

All our children, including children of migrants and minority groups, should grow up learning the language of their home and the language of the society. They need to have a sense of their own identity, whether that is as part of the majority or as part of any of the growing ethnic, cultural, linguistic or religious minorities in this country. Increasingly, we have families not just of minority but of mixed heritage, and children from transnational or culturally and racially diverse families also need to have their multiple identities respected, while having every opportunity to integrate into the life of their school and community and learn to be Irish in new and different ways. Their parents too, especially first-generation immigrants, need to be secure in their employment and able to get permanent residency rights in this country, so that they can start to take their place as voting, active citizens with a voice to be heard and a contribution to make. The majority community also has to learn not only to accept but to welcome people from different cultures and backgrounds, as people who have much to offer our society, culturally and spiritually as well as economically.

All our children must grow up with a clear idea of both their rights and their responsibilities. As they grow to adulthood, they need to develop the ability to engage freely and critically with all aspects of the life of society. And so, when the time comes for our imagined child to go to preschool and later to primary school, it should have a place that is suitable to its needs, preferably at a local school that is adequately resourced to meet the needs of all the community's children, including those with physical or intellectual disabilities, psychological or emotional problems or learning difficulties.

All children – not just those who are lucky enough to be able to afford a wide programme of extracurricular lessons – should get a physical, artistic, moral and spiritual as well as academic education. Our society needs our children to experience a curriculum that makes space for creativity and reflection, for music, art, drama, sport, dance, poetry and storytelling. I would also like to see children learning to be still and to meditate, to reflect and to become socially aware and socially responsible and to develop their sense of compassion – for unless our children are brought up to be responsible and compassionate, we will not be able to sustain a society that is thoughtful and caring in the future, a society that goes on caring for all its people and meeting the needs of future generations with an open heart.

At second level, I hope that all young people in a future Ireland will continue to enjoy school, seeing it as a haven of creativity and a hub of intellectual excitement rather than a place of drudgery and mindless competition. Young people at this age are at their most idealistic and are eager to change the world, yet they are easily soured by a system that they experience as repressing their freedom of expression and inimical to their culture. Education is highly valued in our society, but it is often thought of as an economic rather than a social and a moral good. In a future socially just Ireland, education will be valued for its own sake as well as for the economic benefits that it can bring to society and the individual. Instead of forcing young people through an exam-oriented programme, I wish schools could open youngsters up to their own wonderful possibilities and that their teachers would lead them in exploring and developing their talents. Through treating them with respect and debating issues sensitively with them, teachers should help them to develop a moral compass by which to make responsible decisions. I want the young people of Ireland to grow up with the intellectual and moral equipment to be able to resist the blandishments of the market culture with which they are constantly bombarded and make good choices for themselves and their society, free from consumerist pressures. Young people, given the right kind of support and respect from their parents and teachers, can and will make those good decisions, but it will not happen in a school system that is based on competitive examinations, whose ultimate if unspoken goal is to exclude some students from third level, from employment and from civic life itself.

As our imaginary child emerges from adolescence and starts to think about taking his or her place in the adult world, their needs will change again. The young person needs the first step into adult life that best suits their talents and abilities, whether that is a place in a college or university or a job that allows the young person to use their skills and talents. Not everyone can have a job that is glamorous and thrilling, but everyone should work in a place where they are respected and can respect themselves as contributing to society, where they can earn a decent living wage and where their talents and skills are valued.

Adults' needs also change over time, and at some point everyone needs to avail themselves of services such as housing, continuing education and medical or psychiatric treatment, counselling and support in the face of difficulties they experience in life, such as bereavement, addiction, mental illness, financial difficulty or family breakdown. All of us need to be constantly supported to live the best life we can, as far as possible as part of a community and in the company of family and friends. We must see mental health as part of general health and make provision for good mental health in the same way that we try to provide for good physical health; the stigmatization of mental illness probably explains our society's poor provision in the area of psychiatric health, whether diagnosed in childhood or emerging later in life. Lack of services for mental health is at the root of many of our social problems, including family breakdown, addiction and homelessness, and provision of such services is crucial to the creation of infrastructures that support a socially just society. All citizens should also have access to sports and the arts, as participants or spectators, to community and civic life and to social discourse, public debate and political participation.

As middle age settles on our imaginary citizen of the new, socially just Ireland, they should be able to continue to work for as long as they are willing and able to do so, to look after their dependants, who may now be older family members rather than children, and to plan for retirement and old age. As our citizen gets older, a socially just society would allow them to age at their own pace. Older people have much to offer in the way of experience, advice and other ways of looking at the world, and very often are able to continue to participate in the workplace, as full- or part-time workers or volunteers.

There is much unease in Ireland today about the increasing life-span, which, coupled with declining birth rates and poor pension provision, may lead to a very high dependency ratio in the future, with young people in the workforce having to support more and more older people. Without adequate planning, this changing age profile may indeed pose problems for a future society, but not all old people are or need to be dependent, and many older people in the future will be able to help their younger colleagues to sustain and ease the lives of those who are frail or ill and in need of a high level of care. Again, it is a question of meeting actual needs, rather than assuming that the needs of older people are chronologically determined. As medical science advances and people live longer, they may also be able to live more healthily and more actively for most of their life, and there will doubtless be technological developments that will make this increasingly likely for more and more people.

Technology is a rapidly developing and changing resource whose future impact we can probably not even imagine. Technology is socially neutral: it is up to us to use it either for the common good or for the benefit of the privileged. Used correctly and distributed fairly, technological goods may immeasurably improve all our lives, especially the lives of older people and people with disabilities. On the other hand, technological goods could become one more way of discriminating between those who have access to them and those who are excluded.

A society built on social justice and responsive to the needs of its citizens would provide a variety of options for older people and a continuum of care, depending on the person's developing needs. People should be able to work full-time for as long as they are able and willing to work, perhaps with the option to withdraw gradually from the workplace, working part-time maybe for many years, and gradually reducing their commitment as their circumstances change. Likewise, older people should be supported to live independently for as long as that is their wish, with appropriate household help or nursing or medical services as necessary; with easy access to sheltered or supportive housing, and to hospital and nursing care if they become ill or frail and are no longer able to care for themselves.

If we can agree that every person born into our society deserves what they need, in childhood, youth, adulthood, middle age and old age, then we are signing up to the idea of social justice, because that is in essence what social justice is about: meeting everyone's needs as a right, providing for everyone not according to their income level or social status, their gender, skin colour or cultural identity, but according to their needs and circumstances. As a society, however, we are rather muddled about what it is that we are prepared to provide for our citizens, and about how social goods are to be distributed, and we seem increasingly to be opting for a market model of provision, in housing, in health and even in education.

The market has been good to Ireland: we experienced nothing

less than an economic miracle in the recent past. But the values of the marketplace are limited; excellent as the marketplace may be at providing economic goods, it cannot and must not be entrusted with providing social goods. The marketplace, after all, has no understanding of the concept of social goods, it has no conscience. On the contrary, the rules of the marketplace are based on competition, which in turn is based on greed and exclusion. There is a kind of thinking that says greed is good, because it drives the market. The problem with greed is that it is insatiable, and a society that is so enslaved is bound to be an unhappy society. Greed can never be satisfied; it is a monster that keeps people eternally miserable, no matter how much they own and no matter how much they consume. Greed has no place as an organizing principle of a just society.

We can all recognize the value of a socially just society, where people's needs are met and no one is excluded on the basis of cultural and economic difference, but until we acknowledge our greed and let go of it, we will never attain social justice. We also need to let go of our fear of people who are different from ourselves, of our contempt for people of a different background, and our tendency to blame people for their poverty. We need also to let go of our overweening ambitions for ourselves and our own children at the expense of everyone else.

Divesting ourselves of these negative values – greed, selfishness, fear, contempt, feelings of superiority – and replacing them with values of justice, equity, inclusion and collectivism may seem impossible. We look at how society works and we think: it can't change, we are too closely wedded to our own interests, it's human nature to be competitive and to exclude others, it's just the way things are. But that is not necessarily so. If we are prepared to envision a different way of living, and to articulate that vision and reiterate it over and over again, we can win hearts and minds. It is possible to persuade people to change their views and their ways of living. In the past, people thought that many things would never change and yet they did. Women got the vote, for example, though it must have seemed impossible to most people in the mid-nineteenth century; other enormous changes in gender politics followed, so that now women can own property independently of their fathers and husbands, work in whatever jobs they are suited to, and play their part in the life of society outside the home. On a smaller scale, who ever would have believed ten years ago that Irish people would virtually unanimously and with little argument accept the idea of a ban on smoking in pubs?

As new ideas are discussed and publicly debated, people think about them and see their merits, and gradually, over time, social attitudes change. Some social changes come about as a result of a sudden event or series of events; some come about partly because of legislation or because as a society we sign up to international treaties and agreements such as the Declaration of Human Rights; but in the end social change comes because people want change, they see the value of change and they make a collective decision to accept and to implement it. I believe that my vision of a socially just future for Ireland is not an impossible dream.

It is up to us all, politicians and people, to think about it, talk about it and come up with the mechanisms for bringing about what amounts to a social revolution. We need to overhaul the infrastructures of our society and put in place infrastructures that will support social justice.

Social justice is not, however, a plateau that we can reach, which will then sustain itself: social justice is constantly evolving, and we can bring it about only by making a commitment to it, and by continuing to plan for it into the future. Planning has never been our strong point in this country. We are good in a crisis, we are good at creative solutions to immediate problems, and we have a political system that, for all its merits, unfortunately tends to reward short-term thinking. This is our biggest challenge in this new century: the challenge of changing our way of thinking so that we are not constantly responding to immediate circumstances but have a long-term view and a plan for how we are to achieve our long-term aims. The time has come in our development as a nation to think long and hard about what it is that we want for our society, how we will achieve what it is that we want, and how we can put in place the mechanisms for change. But through it all, we need to keep steadily in view the vision of social justice – the ideal that all our citizens are provided for according to their needs, and that opportunities in life are equally available to all regardless of social circumstances.

If this vision is discussed and debated enough, I am convinced that Irish people will want to embrace and implement it. Our economy may be in tatters, but we have known what it is to be poor and we have known what it is to be rich. We are well placed to see money and the marketplace, consumerism and property, greed and competition and ambition for what they are and especially to see their limitations. For much longer than we were a rich society, we have been a thoughtful society, a soulful society, a resourceful society and a society that values family life, learning and social networking. It is time to pool those values now and re-vision our nation as a socially just society, where all our children are cherished equally, not just by the constitution, but by the nation, the community and all our national structures and institutions, in fact as well as in theory, so that our children can seize their opportunities and go forward to play their role and achieve their potential for the good of us all.

12

Building Sanctuary

For many years I had been turning over in my mind the idea of creating a physical space for meditation and contemplation for myself, one that I could share with others who were seeking rest and inner peace. My dream was of a beautiful space in the middle of the city of Dublin into which you could open a door and find silence, stillness, beauty and rest. A hidden place, a sacred secret space. When Focus Ireland's first supportive housing development, Stanhope Green, was established in the old Sisters of Charity convent in Stanhope Street, the sisters moved into more modest convent accommodation on the site. Later, I moved, with two other sisters, into a house that had been a gate lodge to the convent, at the entrance to what is now Stanhope Green. We wanted to live in community with the residents of Stanhope Green, and we have always valued our connection to our friends and neighbours there. One of the sisters later moved on, and now I live with the remaining sister, Síle Wall, who worked with me from the earliest days of the development of Focus Ireland. Josie

O'Rourke, who is a tenant of Focus Ireland, also spends a lot of time at our house, and is very much a part of our community in the lodge. The gate lodge is situated in Stanhope Street, between the Stanhope Green development and a hostel offering medium-term accommodation to troubled teenagers.

There was some space at the rear of the lodge, and I decided that I would ask the Sisters of Charity for that site to create the place of rest and calm for the mind, body and spirit I had dreamed of: a place of stillness, a sanctuary in the midst of one of the busiest areas of inner-city Dublin. I wanted to create a place that would offer deep peace and serenity, a centre for the sort of meditation, contemplation and reflection that awakens for us the deeper meaning, value and purpose of life – an inward eye in the centre of the storm. I had difficulty in explaining to the Sisters of Charity exactly what I had in mind. I couldn't get the concept across. Again, this was a situation where a solution had to be shown before the problem became clear.

After some persuasion, the sisters agreed to give me the use of half the site. The next big problem was the fact that there was no funding at all for this kind of project. I knew that however difficult it had been to finance the other services I had been involved with, finding funding for this would be even more difficult as it was so new and there were no prototypes for it. So, having gained the co-operation and goodwill of an architect, an engineer and a builder, who offered their services free, in 1998 I embarked, with Sr Síle Wall, on developing this 'cracked' idea of building a sanctuary in the centre of the city, and slowly the funding came. Gradually we managed to construct the buildings

The entrance to the Sanctuary, Dublin, a place of peace and healing, set in the midst of the bustling city.

and establish the garden. We got a number of awards for our garden, which helped to make it known and in turn that helped with funding. It was a very exciting time.

We call it the Sanctuary. In it we have pleasantly furnished, light-filled rooms that we use for meditation and other classes and sessions, as well as some office space, an art therapy centre and a very small sacred space, all set in our magnificent, beautiful meditation gardens. In the Sanctuary we offer programmes and courses on meditation, mindfulness, yoga, t'ai chi and other meditative experiences to the public. I myself participate in the practice and teaching of meditation at the Sanctuary. It also specializes in creating tailor-made programmes on meditation, mindfulness and stillness for children and young people and their teachers and mentors, and for youth leaders and workers.

We live in times of great change and uncertainty, confusion and unease. The pace of life has quickened, and the problems we experience are becoming increasingly difficult and complex. Balancing life and work today makes a huge claim on people's resources – physical, mental and emotional. Many of us have lost our sense of time and place. Time to think, time to reflect, time to grow, time to be present in ourselves, and time to begin a journey towards balancing who we are and what we do. The Sanctuary offers people exactly that: time and space.

It is a place of meditation in contemporary life. The Sanctuary is for everyone – people in all kinds of work and in all kinds of professions and some with no work. We reach out to many people, including teachers and schools, to those working in prison and addiction services or in the homelessness sector, and to volunteers, youth workers, social workers and those with whom they are working, and many others. It is for people of all religions, and of none, people from different cultures. We don't just respect other people's differences, we actively embrace them and view them as a source of richness.

When people visit the Sanctuary, they embark on a journey. They come here for many reasons and it is not our place to question why. We just welcome them. We are a gentle presence on their journey. We offer people the space and time to reconnect with themselves. Meditation enables them to make the changes they want to make and become what they want to be. Through our courses and programmes, we enable people to have a greater awareness and understanding of who they are and how they relate in all aspects of their life. We believe that by enabling people to become more present to themselves, they can reconnect with their environment, culture, family, community and society in a deeper way.

The Sanctuary can be seen in a Christian context, but it is open to all faiths and traditions. We see the wisdom in this diversity and embrace it. It is first and foremost a place of meditation and we recognize that meditation transcends religion and tradition. We acknowledge the thousands of years of wisdom from meditation in different traditions and beliefs – Christianity, Islam, Buddhism, Hinduism, Judaism, Sufism and Taoism. Meditation is an art. It is the art of being aware, of being present, of being in the now, of being grounded. It is the art of being. Meditation is not just about being relaxed: it is about being relaxed and alert at the same time. It is a way of bringing us back to ourselves, where we can really experience our true being beyond our thoughts and emotions.

The Sacred Space – one of the rooms in the Sanctuary.

Meditation brings us home to our true selves, to where the outward surface area of our mind is at one with the deep peace at the core of our being.

Because each person is unique at the Sanctuary, our approach respects the lived experience of everyone. Through sound, meditation, movement, poetry, storytelling, art, discussion, theory and practice we offer a 'way of being' which will lead to a greater balance and harmony in life. When people arrive at the Sanctuary we don't take them on a guided tour. The Sanctuary is there for them to explore – it's part of the journey – and through that they find their own internal sanctuary.

No matter how busy our lives are, we all need moments of mindful awareness. In these moments we can tune into our emotions and thoughts. The Sanctuary is an environment for the senses. The colours, sounds, textures, tastes and smells all help create a sense of awareness. We want the Sanctuary to provide people who come here with opportunities to find sanctuary in their own lives, no matter where they are.

There is no disconnection between a life of action and a life of meditation. Spirituality is not about withdrawing into the self. We believe, on the contrary, that through meditation and mindful awareness it is possible to create a fair and compassionate society. We cannot teach this. What we can do is to create an environment where people can grow into being more compassionate people. At the Sanctuary, we offer an environment that invites people to pause and reflect on their way of being. We offer them an opportunity to come closer to their heart, to be more connected, to be more loving, to have the courage to be more authentic. We believe that will make a different, more caring world. We can't change the world; but we can change ourselves, and that is how greater change begins. Each person can *be* the change they want to see in the world.

In 2010 the Sanctuary held its first major national conference on Mindfulness and Mental Health, followed in 2011 by a conference on Mindfulness and Young People. These are part of a series of annual conferences which the Sanctuary plans to organize. The Sanctuary has a very committed board of directors chaired by Frank Allen. Síle and I continue as directors, and under the direction of Niamh Bruce, we have a team of very skilled staff, facilitators and volunteers.

The Sanctuary welcomes thousands of people each year, who seek peace and quiet, silence and stillness in their lives. This special place is an oasis of restoration and calm at the heart of a capital, and it aims to speak to the hearts of many.

13

Gratitude

The great medieval Christian mystic Meister Eckhart preached that if the only prayer we ever said was 'Thank you', it would be enough. The essence of gratitude is acceptance of what is. It is amazing how much of life we can miss when we lose our sensitivity to wonder and awe. When we simply trudge through our days, we may easily miss the daily gifts of life, and lose our sense of gratitude. When we awaken to what is within us and around us, when we savour, relish and taste life fresh each day, our heart overflows with gratitude.

If we remember the people who have blessed our life we realize many of them may be unaware of what they have done. They may have blessed us with their smiles, their loving looks, their affirmations, their stories, their love, their compassion, their concern and their care. When we become aware of the vast goodness around us and the great blessings that abound, we also become aware of our own need to bless, with our presence, our goodness, our strengths, our healing, our courage, our vitality.

Many people have blessed me during my lifetime. I remember, especially, older people – such as Mrs Connors, a wonderful lady belonging to a Traveller family, who reared a big family of ten and then reared her son's family of ten when their mother died. I met her often and I always felt her presence, and that she was in some way blessing me.

Looking back I recall how, whenever I said goodbye to my ageing father, he would raise his hand as he wished me well, saying *slán girl*. It was only later, when a cousin of mine arrived from the States, that I understood the significance of this gesture. She told me she sensed that when he raised his hand to say goodbye, it was as if he was offering his blessing – which is a lovely thought.

It is often through tragedies or disasters that we can learn something about life's priorities. When we have lost somebody, or a treasure that we have really valued, perhaps an irreplaceable possession, we may reach the realization that life alone is essential. Disasters, tragedies and traumas are great equalizers: they give the opportunity for true humility and gratitude to creep in, the gratitude for simply being alive.

The American essayist Ralph Emerson wrote, 'Never lose the opportunity of seeing anything that is beautiful, for beauty is God's handwriting – a wayside sacrament.' Vincent van Gogh once said, 'The best way to know God is to love many things.' I find that, as I get older, there are numerous opportunities for me to be grateful. This is not the time to moan about how old I am getting, nor is it the time to grieve for my lost youth. This is a time to celebrate and be grateful for having come this far. To be grateful that I am more able than ever to enjoy relationships, memories and recollections. That I have perspective on myself and the world, and enjoy more quiet moments alone. That I am able to give more attention to the inner journey, which is the longest journey of all. Because my life has deepened over the years and has evolved a rich inner vitality made up of memory, insight and confidence, it is now time to appreciate all this and to be grateful. This is a wonderful gift.

I have worked with the poor for over fifty years now, and they have taught me many things, but above all, they have taught me to be grateful. They point out all the good things that have been given to us, and how much we take them for granted. The people I live among in my home at Stanhope Green include many who have experienced homelessness, poverty, depression and exclusion. Over the years, I have had the privilege of sharing with them prayers, liturgies and rituals. What strikes me more than anything else is the extraordinary way in which this group is able to name and claim the moments of grace and gratitude in their lives. They are not calculating or doing cost/benefit analyses of their lives; they are simply acknowledging and recognizing and being grateful for everything they have. Together, we set down small islands of hope, of celebration, to help us keep sight of God's great love. During these liturgies and rituals, I realize very clearly that grace comes to us when we begin to appreciate the goodness that is already ours. Even if what we possess does not include many material goods, once we feel grateful the goods expand – what we have means more to us – and so does our sense of gratitude. Together we are able to acknowledge moments of gratitude for people who walked with us through life, for those who stood beside us when our hopes were small, for those who walked with us when we had nothing but sorrow and death, for those who celebrated our emptiness, acknowledging who we are, for those who broke bread with us and shared with us new life.

When we are grateful, the insignificant becomes significant; the unimportant, important; the smallest gesture takes on a whole new meaning. We know that when we practise gratefulness, everything changes. It is a bright light illuminating a dark room.

Gratitude and greed are mutually exclusive. As mentioned before, greed arises from the belief that we are in control, that we can control everything, and that anything we have we deserve. Greed is a mindset that tells us we must get and get and get. It is the yearning for more, the push to acquire more, win more, own more. Greed does not know the meaning of enough. Those who lack gratitude's vision do not possess things: things possess them, and that is misery. Gratitude flows from a vision of one's life as a reality received, a gift given freely and spontaneously by God.

The poet Rilke, observing the way the anemone flower opens to the morning light, asks, 'When are we ever fully open to receive?' Openness in this sense stands for a basic attitude to life, for a readiness to receive life to the full. This openness is in itself fullness, it is gratitude.

A friend of mine said to me once, 'I know the sunsets are for everyone, but I believe that what each of us receives from a sunset is a personal gift that is uniquely ours.' I was very moved by her words and it became clear to me that so much depends on whether or not we face life with eyes of gratefulness. If instead we face life with a sense of entitlement, then we make demands, set expectations and create rules regarding what we need to be joyful and happy.

This sense of entitlement is one of the major enemies to spiritual growth: it hardens our souls and keeps us from appreciating the gifts we have all been given. A demanding nature can even hurt the very people in our lives who offer gifts to us. It's all about receiving and not taking. There is plenty for all of us – for you and for me – if only we have the eyes to see and the ears to hear and the heart to feel the gifts all around us and within us.

The way to heal a greedy, envious or demanding heart is to replace it with a grateful heart. When gratitude becomes our way of life, we make peace with our greed and with our envy, not excusing it or ignoring it, but acknowledging it as part of ourselves. Then with the Psalmist we can pray: 'It was you who created my innermost being, and put me together in my mother's womb. For all these mysteries, I thank you for the wonder of myself and for the wonder of your works' (Ps. 139: 13–14).

One of the purposes of prayer is to remind us of the gracious generosity of God and to awaken in us a sense of appreciation for the goodness that is already ours. Prayer moves us deeply into the mystery of grace, and opens us to the abundance of God. Here our emptiness becomes a gift rather than a disappointment, as God fills us with love. The more empty we are, the more we know our need for God. And in humility we begin to recognize the gifts and graces bestowed on us over our lifetime.

Gratitude is not just a feeling. It is not enough to feel grateful – we must think grateful, imagine grateful and act grateful. We cannot simply say 'Thank you', and then continue in a demanding, controlling or competitive way. Gratitude is a whole and holy attitude.

Gratitude is at the heart of a healthy spirituality. When we are grateful, our lives begin to change instantly and we see that we have so much more than we previously realized, even during those times when the world would have us think we are poor.

Sometimes it is hard to be grateful for something, because when you admit that something is a gift, you may also, perhaps, admit your dependence on the giver, and quite often there is something within us that bristles at this idea of dependence. And yet you simply cannot make a gift to yourself: not in the truest sense of the word. Yes, you can buy the same thing or even something better for yourself, but then it will not be a gift. Dependence is always there when a gift is given and received. A mother depends on her child for the smallest gift; even though she has given him not only the money he spent on the gift, but his very life, and the upbringing that made him generous.

In the past, people expressed their thanks by saying, 'I'm much obliged.' We hardly ever hear people saying that today, and that is because people don't want to be obliged, don't like acknowledging their dependence on other people.

The greatest gift we can give is thanksgiving. When we make a gift, we often give what we can spare, but in giving thanks, we give ourselves. One who says 'Thank you' to another really says 'We belong together.' The giver and the thanksgiver belong to each other. The bond unites them and frees them from alienation.

And so, when we give from the heart, we are free. To

give thanks means to give expression to mutual belonging. In genuine thanksgiving we are rooted in universal belonging. Wholehearted thanksgiving engages the whole person. Even our sufferings and losses can become occasions of gratitude when we recognize through them the sufferings and losses of others, and also when we realize we are not abandoned, even if we abandon ourselves. Wherever we may be, we are in some way engaged in universal give and take. If our feelings are too scarred and too jaded to vibrate fully with the great giving and receiving, we might at least find one small area in which we can spontaneously respond with joy.

Life is full of surprises, and that is the key to gratitude. Even if our life lacks the surprise of the extraordinary, the ordinary can always be surprising. The surprise of the unexpected wears off, but the surprise of freshness never wears off. In rainbows, it is obvious. Less obvious is the surprise present in the most ordinary things, but we can learn to see it as plainly as we see rainbows. Sometimes we have to train ourselves to spot it. Robert Frost calls it 'a mist from the breath of a wind/ tarnish that goes at a touch of the hand'.

One drop of surprise can lead to oceans of gratefulness. To recognize surprise is the beginning and the source of gratitude: we catch a glimpse of the joy to which gratefulness opens the door. If we knew how the whole world worked, we could still be surprised that there was a universe at all, but if we don't think about it we won't be surprised at it. Our eyes are open to the surprise in the world around us the moment we wake up from taking things for granted.

Gratefulness is the measure of our aliveness. If we are numb, if we take things for granted, then we are dead, because to those who are awake to life's surprises, death lies behind, not ahead. To live life open to surprise, in spite of all that's dying around us, makes us even more alive.

Gratitude keeps us youthful. By being more and more grateful, we get younger every day. Surprise opens our inner eye to the amazing fact that everything is a gift. If nothing can be taken for granted, then we must be grateful. And as we begin to be grateful for small things, our gratitude grows and grows like expanding ripples on the surface of a pool.

Throughout my life, I have had so much to be grateful for, and I have tried to practise gratitude daily. I have developed a habit of writing down in the evening things I am grateful for that day, and the list is endless.

Gratitude helps me to keep perspective and make connections. It is like the sun lighting up the landscape: not a single leaf or blade of grass is different, but everything looks much more attractive. Gratitude helps me to see the proper relationship between things more readily. Gratitude is indispensable on the way to maturity; it helps me to dignify and celebrate life.

At this stage of my life, I want to say, as Dag Hammarskjöld wrote, 'The night is closing in. For all that has been, thanks, for all that is to come, yes.' In Nigeria there is a proverb that says, 'It is the heart that gives and the fingers just let go.' Giving is something only the heart can do and this is true not only of gift-giving but of all forms of giving. The heart knows that all belongs to all.

14

Home to God

I like to think of my life as a journey, a journey from God to God. But actually, there are two journeys that we make in a lifetime: an outward and an inward. My outward journey was into education, work, ministry and service. That outward journey took me from Dingle to Dublin, to Kilkenny and back to Dublin. From home to school to the novitiate, to the service of the poor, in Kilkenny Social Services, Focus Ireland, the Immigrant Council of Ireland, the Young Social Innovators and the Sanctuary, and in each of these I have found a home. But it is by making the second journey, the inward journey, that I find my true home. That is the journey into my true self, the I am, the God within me and around me, in whom I live and move and have my being, and that is the journey I want to try to describe now, my journey into prayer and meditation and towards my ultimate home in God.

These two journeys are of course closely intertwined. They interact with and affect each other all the time. And so it is that when I come to describe the inward journey of the soul, I begin always from my involvement with the poor.

In the mid-1970s, while I was in Kilkenny, Jean Vanier directed us in a retreat, and since then I have visited his L'Arche community in Trosly in France many times, and have become involved with L'Arche communities in Ireland, in particular helping to establish the first L'Arche community in this country, in Kilmoganny, County Kilkenny. Through all this, Jean Vanier has been a spiritual guide to me and a source of inspiration. Through him, and through my involvement with L'Arche, I have deepened my understanding of what I had already begun to learn in Kilkenny about the beauty of those who are neglected by society. I have learned how the poor can be a source of life and healing to me every day of my life. As I walk with them, I have begun to understand better Jesus' relationship with the poor of his time. He said 'Blessed are the poor in spirit', and his whole life demonstrates his love for the poor and his belief that the poor in spirit and the poor who were rejected by society are blessed.

In the story of the cure of the blind beggar, Bartimaeus, we see Jesus putting that principle into action, as he stops to attend to the man's needs. With no ambiguity, very gently, he beckoned the man to come. He was in touch in the deepest way with this blind beggar when he said, 'What do you want me to do for you?'

When we encounter a poor person, outside the church, maybe, or on the street, we may feel awkward or ill at ease. But if we want to be in solidarity with the poor, we need to learn to be with them, to look them in the eye, to treat them as friends. And they know if we are with them. I have begun to see, too, that if I feel a distance from the poor, maybe it is because I have my own agenda.

Maybe I am not able to be with people who are poor, but am looking instead to see what I can do, see what I can fix. Most of us were brought up that way, always wanting to be doing things, looking for success, looking for control, wanting to know the right people. It is a daily struggle for each of us to unlearn those values and to recondition ourselves. Many people hate to see suffering, and they want to change it if they can. There are other people who feel very deeply when they see poverty, and there are others again who want to change the situation in order to feel good in themselves.

Of course, some people are gifted by God to be great doers, but it has been a lifelong struggle to learn that the ability to achieve and to organize are not the only gifts we are given by God. We can learn this from the poor, because they are not interested in competition, they are not interested in who people know; this does not impress them.

The poor challenge me to pray daily to discover my true self, to discover more and more the common humanity we all share. They challenge me to go on this painful journey, questioning my values, striving to be my true self. It is a painful, confusing process. We are all afraid of losing our identity, an identity that we have worked to achieve.

It is very hard to learn the lessons of the poor if your gifts are constantly being rewarded, when your ability to do, to organize, to achieve is being approved and applauded.

The poor constantly challenge me to accept who I am – not what I can do, not what I possess, not what I have done. They challenge me to live more simply. A central question for me and for all Christians today is whether we are open enough to allow the poor to change us – or do we want to change them?

The poor, like Bartimaeus, have a lot to teach us about detachment and fearlessness. He stood up, dropped everything, ran to Jesus. He didn't stop to ask, 'What will people think of me? What will happen to me? What will be asked of me?' He didn't have the baggage that the rest of us carry and that can get in our way when we meet Jesus, or when we meet the poor.

As I walk with Jesus and the poor, I realize how lacking I am in faith and trust, how slow I am to believe in the unconditional love of God and how slow I am to believe in miracles. The poor, like Bartimaeus, are full of faith and trust. When Jesus said, 'What do you want me to do for you?' the blind man said, 'I want to see again.' He hadn't the slightest doubt or the slightest hesitation. This was his deepest desire. I find the same with the poor people I meet. They come to me and they are quite clear: 'I want a house', 'I want respect', 'I want a job', 'I want a life for my children', 'I want peace of mind', 'I want to feel wanted', 'I want to feel I belong'.

They have no doubts about what is their deepest desire. Like Bartimaeus, they are ready for the miracle, they are ready to be utterly transformed.

Our deepest desire as human beings is to know that we are loved, that we are loved absolutely and totally and unconditionally. Through this awareness we, too, will be able to love unconditionally, to go out to others and make sacrifices for others. Jesus is waiting to give us this gift of love, the gift of our true selves, who are made in the image of God.

As I walk with Jesus and the poor, I have come to see in a new way that my weakness is my strength. While I was executive director of Focus Point (later Focus Ireland), a big, busy organization, and at the same time trying to help my family to care for my elderly father, I found it extremely difficult to accept that I had to stop, that I had to take rest, that I was not going to be the person who was in charge of everything. Another reason for my distress was that my mother had died just three days before Focus Point was supposed to open for the first time (in the end it opened two weeks after she died). She suffered from dementia and spent most of the last year of her life in hospital. Her short-term memory was almost totally gone and she lived mostly in the past, in her young days. We conversed in Irish a lot of the time because that was her first language, and watching her move into that stage of her life was very painful. At the beginning she knew she was slipping away and it distressed her. Later, she used to say what could be regarded as funny or foolish things – but I could never think they were funny, I simply couldn't accept that she was losing her mind. In fact, I cried every time I saw her because I found it distressing to see my mother in this sad situation. It was as if this was all happening to me.

In the latter part of her life – the last three months – she communicated less and less. And while her death was rather sudden, it was after all expected and we were, in a sense, prepared for it. It wasn't until about three months later that it really struck me that my mother had gone. Before that, I hadn't given myself time to grieve, partly because I knew I had work to do – and the opening of Focus was a major thing – so the loss of my mother and its meaning came later for me. It was a difficult time, but I sensed her presence, largely because of who she was, but also because of

At home in Lispole with my father, 1989, the year before he died.

the opening of Focus; it was as if she was with me because she knew how important this was to me and wanted to help and support me. After my father died, I also felt his presence. Like my mother, he spent the last year of his life in the local hospital and later in a nursing home. He never settled down in either place because he missed his home, his freedom and the wide open spaces that he loved. And when he died I felt a part of me also died, for it wasn't just the loss of him that I felt, but the loss of my own home. My siblings had their own homes and families, but the family home was the only true home I had ever known. Whilst the house is still there, and it was left to all of us in my parents' will to use while we were alive, the fact that they were gone still left a huge gap that was never to be filled again. Even now, all these years later, when I return to the house, I feel their absence.

Looking back, I can see that the stress of my father's illness and my heavy workload resulted in me becoming totally drained and I grew more and more ill until, finally, I had to give in and stop everything. I felt that I was on the edge, afraid to look to the right or to the left, lest I fell into a dark abyss. I felt a sense of helplessness and powerlessness that I had never known before. It was a dark, dark, Good Friday experience.

It seemed to last for ever, but in fact it was only for five or six weeks. Today I can say that it was one of the most important times of my life. A way was opened in me to a new understanding, a new sensitivity and a new hope that made space for my own fragility and the fragility of the most forlorn and the most broken of human beings. As I got well, I began to understand my own humanity. My illness helped me to connect my frailty and brokenness with the brokenness of the world in a totally new way.

It was during that time that I discovered in a new way the practice of meditation and mindfulness. Meditation had always been part of my life, but in the past it meant reflection, using my mind to reflect on the life of Christ, and I still do that. But the practice of meditation now took on a new meaning. It was learning the Art of Being Still. It was moving beyond my thoughts and emotions to taste and experience my true self: where I was at one with the deepest peacefulness at the core of my being. And this for me is where God dwells. I found this meditation to be of enormous help. It became very important in my life then, and has done since then. It has helped me to live in the present and in the moment, accepting my situation as it is. It has helped me to grow in the realization that though I was suffering, I could still be with situations of suffering and not be overwhelmed by them. It has also helped me to discover an inner strength and an inner peace and stillness. But I know that meditation is an art which takes a lifetime to learn, through consistent practice.

The practice of mindfulness – or mindful awareness – also became a very important part of my life then, and since then. The term 'mindfulness' comes from the Buddhist tradition, and mindfulness is practised widely amongst Buddhists, and now by people of other faiths and beliefs and traditions. The practice of mindfulness brings us into the silence and stillness of our inner world. It helps to give us the ability and the skills to create a safe, quiet space within us, where we can be ourselves, listen deeply to ourselves, and be with ourselves as we are, with acceptance and compassion. Through mindfulness, we see our struggles, our worries, our joys and accomplishments as they are, not more or less important than they are. They are all aspects of life, in the stillness and silence. The practice of mindfulness helps us to live our lives with a sense of calmness, peacefulness, groundedness, realizing that we always have choice. There is also a Christian practice which goes back many centuries, known as the Sacrament of the Present Moment. It means being fully present in the moment, and being conscious of God's presence. This is not so well known today, but it was very much part of our training in my novitiate. That practice prepared me for mindfulness, but mindfulness carried me deeper and helped me to discover an inner strength, and an inner peace and stillness at the core of my being where God dwells. Mindfulness and meditation compliment and affect each other. The practise of mindfulness in daily life helps my meditation, and meditation helps me to be more mindful. Mindful of my own Christian tradition of meditation, contemplation and prayer, I am also eager to learn from others. I believe the time is right now for all of us to learn from different cultures and religions, all that is helpful and that moves us towards a simpler life, a deeper life and a more authentic life in which the inner experience of God is primary, energizing and centring.

Mindfulness, or mindful awareness, is knowing what we're doing while we're doing something, and accepting things as they are. To me it is a way of being in the present, and a way of being in God, because God is always in the present. I believe the whole universe is permeated by God. God is everywhere. Everybody and everything is in God.

Later I had a somewhat similar experience of stress, but I dealt with it differently, because of my meditation and practise of mindfulness. From my own poverty and weakness I had learned that no matter how oppressed I may be, I always retain some capacity to choose light over darkness. I can choose to risk opening myself to goodness or to give in to the power that oppresses me. The choice is up to me. When we take risks, when we let the props go and give ourselves up to the struggle, our gifts and potential grow more radiant.

I see my life as a life of service to God and of the poor. But I know too that in my life of service there was a lot of ego. In the past I wanted to gain the approval of others — and even the approval of God. What I didn't realize then was that because I didn't accept and love myself, I could not love anybody else. I was sensitive and caring, but did not consider myself good enough. And in my relationships with people, and even with God, I did not consider myself worthy to be loved. But over time, I learned and am still learning to realize God's unconditional love, and am making that an anchor in my life. I am learning that I don't have to prove to God who I am, or what I do for him, because I am already precious and unconditionally loved. I often repeat over and over to myself the words of Isaiah 43: 'I have called you by name, you are mine, you are precious in my eyes. I love you — I have created you for my glory.'

I remind myself of Jesus' assurance that I am more precious than the birds of the air, the lilies of the field.

> Look at the birds of the air;
> They do not sow or reap or store away in barns,
> And yet your heavenly Father feeds them.
> Are you not much more valuable than they?
>
> Matthew 6: 26

I use scripture over and over again to assert my personal identity. I realize it is no longer my love of God, it is God's love for me and in me that matters.

I cannot discuss my spiritual journey without discussing prayer, which is the language through which this relationship with God is communicated and deepened. Prayer has developed for me from finding God, to a way through which God finds me. Prayer is a means – not an end in itself. Prayer is a way of deepening my relationship with God.

To pray is to live in communion with the Divine. It is not just the raising of the heart and mind to God, it is the raising of our whole being – body, breathing, bones, blood, head, hands and feet; keeping nothing back from God. It is being present to God with the whole person: body, mind and spirit. It is the Divine taking possession of us. We can never achieve prayer – it is always received as a gift. In prayer I open to God who I am, and God gazes on me with the creative and transforming eye of love. Prayer is God's work – it is a handing over to God.

Prayer is not just spending time with God. It is not static, it is dynamic. Authentic prayer changes us. It strips us and indicates where growth is needed. Authentic prayer is never complacent. Authentic prayer disturbs us. Authentic prayer can make us uneasy at times, as it leads us to self-knowledge and to humility.

I pray to expand my experience of God. Thomas Aquinas tells us that 'God is always bigger than what we can think about God.' St Augustine tells us: 'Anyone who says he has understood God knows nothing about God.' We do not need Aquinas or Augustine to tell us that – common sense tells us that God is always bigger than anything we can know of God, and deeper than any experience we can have of the Divine. God is always bigger than whatever we think about, or how we relate to God at any one time. Prayer is a means to expand our concept and our experience of God. That is the purpose of prayer, and it is the purpose of Life itself. The realization of the Divine and finding our identity in the Divine.

As I have said, I find that prayer is not about finding God, it is about allowing God to find me, in whatever way and form God is working in my life.

Similarly when I minister to people through my work or teaching or writing, it is not that I communicate God, it is that I make myself available to God – so that God will be able to work in me, and through me to affect others. I am not in control of what happens. I used to think that I was communicating God's love in my message, now I know that this is not so. This is God's work. I do not take on God's responsibility: my part is to let myself go in God, and let God work in me and through me. I am confident in the God that I believe in. I am confident that God is at work in me.

I began in my prayer life and my relationship with God by talking to God; believing that God listened. At that stage I believed I could bring all my needs to God, trusting that what I could not do or others couldn't do for me – God would do. I still do that. But as I grew in my spiritual life silent meditation became very important in my life, as I said earlier. This is very much a prayer from my heart. God is now not an idea or a symbol, but – when I concentrate on my breath or mantra, leading to silence – God is a prevailing presence. This is silence. Sometimes the silence is deep, and full of presence. Being present to 'The Presence'. In this experience of presence, there is love, trust and abandonment. It is a time of dying to the masks and to the false self. Here there is no place for falsity and dishonesty. Many times, though, this silence is empty, a sense of nothingness, and staying with it is an act of deep faith.

Prayer/meditation is opening the heart, mind, body and spirit to God. And it is going beyond all the limited processes of the rational mind and opening the mind, body and spirit to the transcendent reality. This demands devotion and self-surrender. It is only when we surrender the Ego (the separate self) that we can turn to God to receive the light which we need to understand him at a deeper level. The mystery of God is the ultimate truth, and this mystery is known by love. Love is going out of one's self, surrendering one's self. It is not something we can achieve ourselves, it is something that comes when we let go. Letting the Divine mystery take possession of us. And at times I have glimpses of this.

I believe that when I am fully present to the now, when I am living in awareness, I am living and experiencing eternal time. I am living and experiencing God. Because this moment, now, is part of every moment from the beginning of time. This moment is part of every moment until the end of time. And when I am fully present here and now, this place is part of everywhere. And so, too, I am part of everywhere. So this prayer is being fully 'I', fully 'now' and fully 'here', and it becomes a way of life.

I believe also that any time I am fully present to anything it is a prayer. The situation does not have to be religious. Every mundane activity that draws my full attention is prayer. Another way of looking at this is to live every moment and do everything consciously and mindfully and in awareness. Mindful awareness helps us to do precisely this. As infants and small children, we are in a state of mindfulness. We have only to watch a small child, concentrating on something like a piece of fluff – totally focused, really present. As we get older, our thoughts and our emotions take over and we lose that mindfulness; we become judgemental and non-accepting. The challenge, therefore, is to try to recapture that innocent acceptance, relearn simple practices of mindful awareness in our daily lives.

The practice of mindfulness on a daily basis, paying proper attention to detail with sensitivity, will help us to achieve this awareness. Everything happens in the present, and yet so many of our moments go unnoticed.

Each breath is precious, supporting life moment by moment. Our thoughts are not us. Our emotions are not us. Yet most of our time is spent repeating stories and thought patterns. Fear, worry and anxiety intrude on our awareness and separate us from the unfolding experience of life. We develop habits of inattention and distraction, and absent-mindedness. Modern culture actively encourages us to practise *not* being present in our own lives, which to me is a great shame.

I have found that the practice of living consciously and mind-fully seeds, fuels and supports my prayer and meditation, and vice versa. The practice of living mindfully and consciously can take place in any aspect of my life. When I eat mindfully or consciously, nothing else matters to me while I am eating. The food gets my full attention. I eat slowly and pay attention to how the food tastes in my mouth. I am curious about the ingredients. I eat as if I was eating for the first time and the last time and the only time. When I do this I experience the fullness of life and it is a prayer.

I can have the same experience when I walk with mindful

'At times the work I have undertaken has been daunting, and has even appeared impossible . . . But I always knew that if this work was right, it would develop and grow and would be supported, that if it was God's work, nothing could stop it.' (Photo by Derek Speirs)

awareness or consciously and with full attention. Or when I meet people, meeting them as if I was meeting them for the first time, last time and only time. In recent years I walk a lot. I only use public transport or the car when I really have to, and I find that walking can be a deeply prayerful and mindful experience; in tune with my rhythmic breathing or a sacred word or phrase.

The practice of conscious living is not something I have attained, but something I aspire to at all times. And when I do practise it, living here and now without concern for past or future, I feel fully alive and it helps me not only spiritually: it helps me to live a healthy psychological and emotional life as well.

So the practice of mindfulness – of being fully 'I', fully 'now' and fully 'here' – is a way of life. A way of living out my true self, my true divine identity, which turns all into prayer.

The spiritual journey is finding all things in God, and God in all things. It is to live freely and gracefully in harmony with the universe. It is noticing more keenly who and what is around. It is being part of the life of all beings and things.

At times the work I have undertaken has been daunting, and has even appeared impossible, especially when I started new projects, new activities or new research and there was little or no funding, and very little support at first. But I always knew that if this work was right, it would develop and grow and would be supported, that if it was God's work, nothing could stop it. This is where my faith in Divine Providence came in. I knew that providence would provide if the work was right, and this was true in all my work – in Kilkenny and in Focus, and later in the Sanctuary, in ICI and

YSI. It was often a joke, amongst the boards of directors with whom I worked, that Stan had her own bank that she relied on. They are joking, but I know it is true.

I have had moments of desolation, when I have been full of opposition to everything, when the things that give joy to other people seem to delude and deceive me. When I pay attention to the poor, the rejected, the homeless, I will see people like myself who are trying to form sentences, who are trying to articulate their pain and find a way of coping with the madding crowd, with the terrible noise, with the stress of insecurity. These people awaken in me an awareness of my homelessness, my own brokenness, my own need for stillness, my own poverty, when the silence of the night tells me about our human condition. It is through these people that I can find parts of myself that have been lost or buried in the past – a time when my vulnerability had been all too obvious.

In my homelessness of the soul, I can hear the voice of God inviting us 'to make your home in me', and it is that invitation, that promise and hope that makes my homelessness tolerable. I can endure it because I know that, ultimately, I have a home, a home that will be revealed; but in order to reach that ultimate home, I need first to realize, to recognize and to experience my spiritual homelessness and to acknowledge and embrace it.

My faith and my work with the poor have taught me the importance of non-violence and the importance of facing my own violence. It is only when we confront the conflict, the violence and the anger in ourselves that we can truly know ourselves, and be truly at peace with ourselves. We can only become filled with peace if we first acknowledge our own propensity to violence and conflict and learn from it.

When I was younger, I was very much driven by anger with the situations I found, particularly the way poor people were treated. I was also angry with anyone who appeared to me not to be interested in creating a more just and caring society. I was intolerant of any display of wealth or anything ostentatious. And this took me time to work through. I needed to learn to accept people as they were, while at the same time holding fast to my own values. In fact, it was only when I took time to examine what was happening in my own heart, and how much my resolve to 'put things right' was driving me on, that I began to see how much unrest I had within myself. My inner life, I realized, was a microcosm of the world, being fuelled by anger and self-righteousness.

This does not mean that I am not still angry. Of course I feel angry when I think about the fact that two billion people in the world today do not have safe drinking water; when I think how hundreds of millions of the world's people are hungry; when I discover that in every city in the world there are women and children being bought, sold, prostituted, abused, rejected, neglected; when I allow myself to remember that in any night in Dublin, the capital of my own country, there are men, women and children homeless and on the streets. Injustices like these make me angry, but I realize now that it is how I deal with that anger, and continue to work for peace and justice, that is important.

Despite all our conflicts, our differences, our disagreements, ugly and brutal and violent though they often are, we have to hold on to the idea that we are all human; even with deep differences, we are all God's children, and that means we are all essentially one.

As I walk with Jesus and the poor, I learn the deeper meaning of community. Stanhope Green, where I live, at one level provides living accommodation for people who would otherwise be homeless. At another level, we are a community of people with a wide range of potentials and needs, people who are sick and well, able and disabled. We all share a single space and time. We meet, touch, embrace and learn more about each other daily. We share a sacred space – a sanctuary and sanctuary garden – where we replenish our minds and hearts and spirits, all the time learning more about the uncertainties, inconsistencies and ambiguities of our lives.

I have learned that for a community to work it takes effort. It takes time and it takes commitment. Its growth and evolution depend on the efforts and commitment of each of us. It means accepting each other's oddities, idiosyncrasies and weaknesses and accepting and acknowledging and facing everything that produces friction or conflict among us.

I have discovered the importance of silence and solitude. I have learned how to be alone within the community and that my deepest self is born in silence, and the individual wisdom of my innermost being is replenished in silence.

These are the gifts we bring and offer to our community, and these are the gifts we receive in community. Stanhope Green has helped me to begin to resolve that pull between a fast life whizzing past and the desire to slow down and to live each moment more fully.

I have experienced the great challenge of living close to people who are or have been oppressed or marginalized. Living in Stanhope Green, I cannot ignore the pain of our neighbours. The daily reality of inner-city life is present all the time. Young people who are lost and lonely, people without homes, families broken or breaking up, troubled people with innumerable problems – all are part of our daily life. I am constantly challenged by the loneliness, the pain, the sadness, the poverty, the oppression of those living around me.

Living close to oppression opens us up to a new understanding and a new compassion. Hardness of heart cannot be maintained for long when faced with such obvious human suffering. I know that it is only when my eyes have been opened and my heart softened by the poor that I am really ready to begin work with the poor and ready to change the circumstances of their lives.

God identifies with the poor not because they are more noble but because they are more vulnerable. Those of us who are not poor are much less vulnerable. Being close to the poor helps me to remove my heart of stone and replace it with a heart of flesh. It helps me to see myself as I really am, to see my intolerances, my impatience, my attachment to security, status and privileges. It shows me my weak human nature. Above all, it forces me to search for the meaning of life and what I am called to be. This is not easy. It is a call to a radical conversion of my heart and mind.

Right through my life my deepest desire has been to become a loving person, living in the unconditional love of God. This desire has always been accompanied by struggle – the struggle of my own human frailty. Daily I have seen and said with Paul, 'The spirit is willing but the flesh is weak.'

In the midst of all this I have found consolation in a deep inner peace, a peace that 'the world cannot give'. I have found consolation too in very strong, supportive friends, among them the poor and marginalized, who have loved, inspired, accepted and challenged me in different ways: Mary Aikenhead, Bishop Birch, Jean Vanier and L'Arche also stand out as central and powerful sources of inspiration and support, reminding me again and again that my strengths are my weaknesses, my weaknesses are my strengths, and if I abide in Christ I will 'bear much fruit'.

As I walk with Jesus and the poor, I am given a clearer sense of the meaning of home and homelessness. Perhaps the greatest gift of the poor has been to reveal to me my own homelessness, my own poverty, my own human fragility and my deep desire to be at home with myself, with other people and with God. I have experienced times when I am not at home within myself. To be out of home in our heart at this level is to be a stranger to love. We are all homeless in our heart when we feel rejected, when we feel we are not known and not loved, not precious, when our image of ourselves is poor. There is something within every human spirit that does not relish that land of homelessness, yet too much companionship and security covers over the rawness of reality and prevents us from encountering the mystery of our inner homelessness. Our homelessness is a secret territory in which we can discover our true selves.

Throughout my life, God has spoken to me through my weakness and brokenness. Life has broken me in many ways. Physically, through exhaustion and sickness. Emotionally, through relationships, loss and hurt by situations and people.

Spiritually I have been broken by fear, guilt and anxiety. But through the cracks in my life, when I was open to it, God's radiance shone.

Life taught this to me: when I was open and allowed the radiance of God to shine through my weaknesses, I realized that the presence and breath of God that resides within can only shine through the cracks. The more I surrendered, the more I was able to let go of false images of myself, and see and accept myself as I really was – vulnerable, weak, afraid, anxious. And once I began to accept and realize this, I began also to realize that God wanted to meet me there, in my brokenness – and that I could only really let God in through those broken parts of me. This was not something I could have done by myself. It only happens when I let God take over. And that is how it is that the radiance of God lights my way – and leads me safely down the road home.

Index